Stitch by Stitch

Volume 12

TORSTAR BOOKS

NEW YORK · TORONTO

Stitch by Stitch

TORSTAR BOOKS INC.
300 E.42ND STREET
NEW YORK, NY 10017

Knitting and crochet abbreviations

approx = approximately	in = inch(es)	sl st = slip stitch
beg = begin(ning)	inc = increas(e)(ing)	sp = space(s)
ch = chain(s)	K = knit	st(s) = stitch(es)
cm = centimeter(s)	oz = ounce(s)	tbl = through back of
cont = continue(ing)	P = purl	loop(s)
dc = double crochet	patt = pattern	tog = together
dec = decreas(e)(ing)	psso = pass slipped	tr = triple crochet
dtr = double triple	stitch over	WS = wrong side
foll = follow(ing)	rem = remain(ing)	wyib = with yarn in
g = gram(s)	rep = repeat	back
grp = group(s)	RS = right side	wyif = with yarn in front
dc = half double	sc = single crochet	yd = yard(s)
crochet	sl = slip	yo = yarn over

A guide to the pattern sizes

		10	12	14	16	18	20
Bust	in	32½	34	36	38	40	42
	cm	83	87	92	97	102	107
Waist	in	25	26½	28	30	32	34
	cm	64	67	71	76	81	87
Hips	in	34½	36	38	40	42	44
	cm	88	92	97	102	107	112

Torstar Books also offers a range of acrylic book stands, designed to keep instructional books such as *Stitch by Stitch* open, flat and upright while leaving the hands free for practical work.

For information write to Torstar Books Inc., 300 E.42nd Street, New York, NY 10017.

Library of Congress Cataloging in Publication Data
Main entry under title:

Stitch by stitch.

Includes index.
1. Needlework. I. Torstar Books (Firm)
TT705.S74 1984   746.4   84-111
ISBN 0-920269-00-1 (set)

98765432

© Marshall Cavendish Limited 1984

Printed in Belgium

ISBN 0–920269–12–5   (Volume 12)

Contents

Crochet / COURSE 52

*Patchwork crochet
*Borders
*Diagonal strips
*Joining pieces together
*Pattern for a geometric patchwork rug

Patchwork crochet

There are many different ways of creating exciting and colorful patchwork fabrics with crochet, either by working different shapes and sewing them together or by working strips of fabric using stripes and blocks of color to create the patchwork effect.

Triangles, diamonds, hexagons, square motifs and even circles are just some of the shapes you can crochet to create patchwork fabrics. Strips and blocks of single crochet can also be sewn together. Perhaps the simplest crochet patchwork is formed by making either single crochet squares worked in rows, or granny square motifs worked in rounds (see Volume 3, page 9) in a variety of colors. These can then be sewn together to make a colorful bedspread, afghan or shawl.

If you intend to use a variety of shapes to make the fabric, it is a good idea to plan your design first on graph paper, so that you can see roughly how the different shapes will fit together. When planning this sort of patchwork, it is better to rely on the shapes rather than color to create the patchwork effect, since a large number of colors would detract from the design. When only one shape is to be used you can work with as many colors as you like, provided that they complement each other when sewn together.

Borders

Once patchwork pieces have been sewn together, a border should be worked all the way around the patchwork to make sure that the edges of the fabric are neat and even where the different pieces have been joined.

You can work single crochet or half doubles around the fabric, working just one row or several rows in different colors, depending on the yarn used and the effect you want to achieve. A deep fringe knotted all the way around the edge of your patchwork makes an ideal trimming for a shawl or bedspread.

Simon Butcher

Diagonal strips

Strips worked at an angle give added interest to a completed patchwork fabric The effect depends upon distinctive shaping, but the strips are simple to work. Use a bulky knitting so the shaping is prominent.

1 Make 2 chains for the first corner. Work a single crochet into the 2nd chain. Turn. Make 2 chains and work a single crochet into the 2nd of these 2 chains for the first increase. Do not count the turning chain as a stitch.

2 Work a single crochet into the next stitch. Increase at the end of the row by working a single crochet into the loop on the edge of the work, placing the hook downward and under the loop to make a neat edge.

continued

5

3 Turn. Increase at the beginning and end of each row in the same way until there are 9 stitches (not counting the turning chain) to form the side edge. For a wider strip increase to the width required.

4 Start to work diagonally across the fabric. Increase a stitch as before at the beginning of the next row. Work across the next 7 stitches and work the last 2 stitches together (see Volume 2, page 4) to decrease a stitch.

5 Turn. Make 1 chain and work the first 2 stitches together to decrease. Work to the end of the row and increase a stitch by working into the side loop as before. 9 single crochets.

6 Continue to shape the sides in this way, decreasing at one end and increasing at the other end on every row until the strip is the length required. Finish the last row with a decrease, then turn the work.

7 Now square the end of the strip. Make 1 chain. Work across the next 7 stitches. Now turn, thus decreasing a stitch at this end of the row.

8 Make 1 chain. Decrease 1 stitch as before at the beginning of the row. Work across the next 4 stitches. Work the next 2 stitches together so one stitch has been decreased at each end of row.

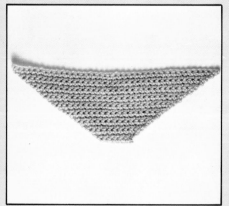

9 Continue to decrease in this way until all the stitches have been worked off and the end of the fabric is square as shown.

10 To work this bucket shape start with 7 chains and work 6 single crochets (not counting the turning chain) into the chain. Increase a stitch at each end of every row, using the same method as given for the strip, until there are 38 stitches, then fasten off.

11 Work the first part of this diamond in the same way as for the strip until there are 9 single crochets in all.

12 Decrease a stitch at each end of the row, as for the strip, until only 3 stitches remain.

13 Work 1 row, then skip the first stitch and work the last 2 stitches together as before to complete the diamond.

14 Here we show you a sample in which these 3 different shapes have been sewn together, making a square to be used as the basis for a patchwork fabric.

Joining pieces together

Patchwork pieces are usually overcast together on the wrong side of the work using the same yarn or a matching yarn in a finer ply. If the yarn is very thick, such as rug wool, it may be difficult to work a seam which does not show on the right side of the work.

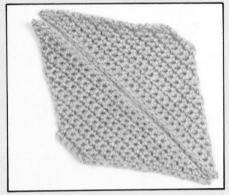

1 Use two strands of the same yarn or use a finer yarn in a matching color and place the pieces to be joined face down, with the top or bound-off edges together so that the stitches correspond.

2 Join the yarn to the bottom right-hand corner of one piece. Take the needle under the outer strand of the first stitch, over the joining and under the outer strand of the corresponding stitch on the other side.

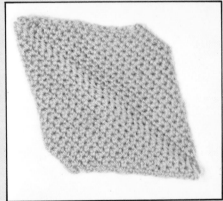

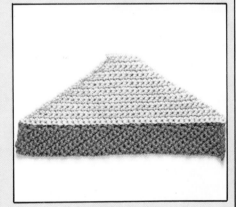

3 Continue to overcast the pieces together in this way so that you are joining only the outer loop of each stitch all the way along the seam.

4 On the right side of the work the two unjoined edges of the stitches lie together, creating an invisible seam.

5 Where you need to join a side edge to the top edge, work in the same way, taking the outer loop of the single crochet on the top edge together with the outer loop on the side of the fabric. Here we show you the right side of the fabric.

Mike Berend

Geometric patchwork rug

Inspired by Italian mosaic tiles, this patterned rug consists of geometric shapes worked in solid colors. Choose a color combination to match your room.

Size 60in (152cm) square.

Materials
  Rug yarn
  110oz (3100g) in main color (A)
  *39oz (1100g) in 1st contrasting
    color (B)*
  *22oz (600g) in 2nd contrasting
    color (C)*
  Size 15 (9.00mm) crochet hook
  Large-eyed carpet needle

Gauge
9 sts and 10 rows to 4in (10cm) worked on size 15 (9.00mm) hook.

1st motif
Using size 15 (9.00mm) hook and A, make 7ch.
Base row (WS) 1sc into 2nd ch from hook, 1sc into each ch to end. Turn.
Next row 2ch, 1sc into 2nd ch from hook —1sc increased—, 1sc into each of next

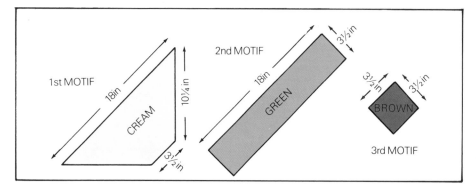

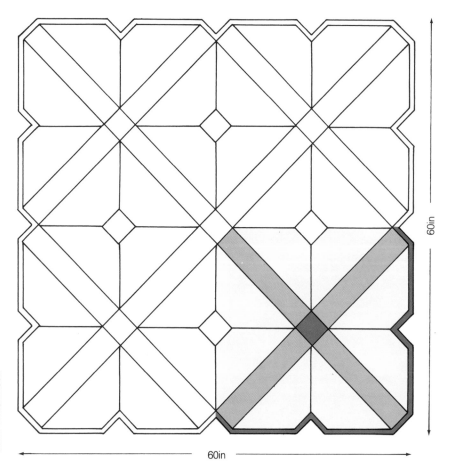

6 sts, 1sc into the loop at edge of work—1sc increased.
Turn.
Rep last row 15 times more. 38sc.
Fasten off. Make 31 more motifs in same way.

2nd motif

Using size 15 (9.00mm) hook and B, make 2ch.
Base row 1sc into 2nd ch from hook. Turn.
1st row 2ch, 1sc into 2nd ch from hook—1sc increased—, 1sc into next st, 1sc into the loop at edge of work—1sc increased. Turn. 3sc.
2nd row 2ch, inc 1sc, 1sc into each of next 3 sts, inc 1sc. Turn. 5sc.
3rd row 2ch, inc 1sc, 1sc into each of next 5 sts, inc 1sc. Turn. 7sc.
4th row 2ch, inc 1sc, 1sc into each of next 7 sts, inc 1sc. Turn. 9sc.
5th row 2ch, inc 1sc, 1sc into each of next 7 sts, (insert hook into next st, yo and draw a loop through) twice, yo and draw through all 3 loops on hook—1sc decreased. Turn. 9sc.
6th row 1ch, dec 1sc, 1sc into each of next 7 sts, inc 1sc. Turn. 9sc.
Rep the 5th and 6th rows 10 times more, then work the 5th row again.
28th row 1ch, dec 1sc, 1sc into each of next 7 sts. Turn. 8sc.
29th row 1ch, dec 1sc, 1sc into each of next 4 sts, dec 1sc. Turn. 6sc.
30th row 1ch, dec 1sc, 1sc into each of next 2 sts, dec 1sc. Turn. 4sc.
31st row 1ch, (dec 1sc) twice. Turn. 2sc.
32nd row 1ch, dec 1sc. Fasten off.
Make 15 more motifs in the same way.

3rd motif

Using size 15 (9.00mm) hook and C, make 2ch. Work as for 2nd motif until the 4th row has been worked. 9sc.
5th row 1ch, dec 1sc, 1sc into each of next 5 sts, dec 1sc. Turn. 7sc.
6th row 1ch, dec 1sc, 1sc into each of next 3 sts, dec 1sc. Turn. 5sc.
7th row 1ch, dec 1sc, 1sc into next sc, dec 1sc. Turn. 3sc.
8th row 1ch, work 1sc into each of next 3 sts. Turn.
9th row 1ch, skip first sc, dec 1sc. Fasten off.
Make 8 more motifs in the same way.

To finish

Sew in all ends. Divide yarn in half and sew motifs tog as shown on page 7; foll chart on left for position of motifs and direction of sts.

Edging

With WS facing work a row of sc evenly around outer edge, working 2sc into corners of 1st motifs and working 2sc tog at base of each V shape. Turn.
Next row Work 1sc into each st all around. Fasten off.

Chris Harvey

Crochet / COURSE 53

- *Crochet with beads
- *Threading beads on the yarn
- *Working single crochet with beads
- *Working half doubles with beads
- *Working doubles with beads
- *Stitch Wise: bead patterns
- *Pattern for a beaded sweater

Crochet with beads

There are many different kinds of beads which can be incorporated into crochet patterns, introduced into the fabric while you are working instead of being sewn on the fabric after the garment has been completed.

The beads are available from most notions departments and specialized craft shops in a variety of materials including plastic, glass and wood, and in various shapes, including round, oval and tubular. Any of these beads can be used with crochet, but make sure that the hole at the center is large enough to allow you to thread them onto your yarn easily. Make sure that the beads you choose for a particular design are not too heavy for your fabric, or they will pull the crochet fabric out of shape, especially if you are working a heavily beaded pattern. Remember that the finer the yarn you are using, the smaller and lighter the beads should be.

The beads can be used in many different ways: For example, work the beads at intervals across the fabric to create a scattered effect as part of a lace pattern, or work them close together to create an encrusted effect for beaded edgings. Motifs can be worked out on graph paper, using different colors and shapes to make flowers or abstract designs which can be used to trim the pocket or bodice of a summer top or evening cardigan.

Heavily-beaded patterns can be used for bags or evening purses, since the fabric in this case can be lined so that the beads do not pull it out of shape. Try combining bright-colored wooden beads and thick cotton or string to make a really unusual tote bag.

Once you know how to work the beads in conjunction with all the basic crochet stitches, you should have no difficulty in combining beads and many crochet

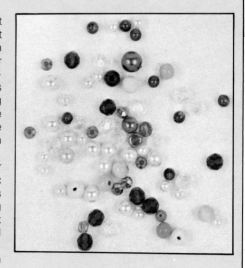

patterns to create attractive and unusual designs of your own.

Threading beads on the yarn

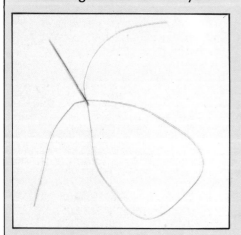

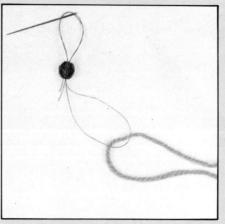

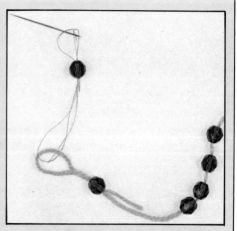

1 Use this method when the hole at the center of the beads is too small to be threaded directly onto the yarn with a needle. Thread ordinary sewing thread into a fine sewing needle so that both ends of the thread pass through the eye of the needle.

2 Loop the yarn to be used for the crochet through the thread loop. Now thread the first bead onto the needle, taking it down over the thread loop.

3 Slide the bead down the thread and over the two strands of yarn. When threading a number of beads onto the yarn, keep one bead over the double strand of crochet yarn to hold it in place while you thread the beads.

Working single crochet with beads

Beads can be worked with either the right or wrong side of the work facing; in each case, a different technique ensures that the beads lie on the right side of the fabric. To duplicate this sample, use a small, round bead with a hole large enough to take a sport yarn.

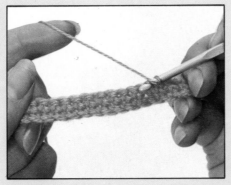

1 Make 32 chains and work 2 rows of single crochet with 31 stitches in each row. Now work the first 3 stitches (including the turning chain) of the next row. Insert the hook through the next stitch from back to front.

2 Wind the yarn over the hook and draw it through the stitch. Now push the bead as close to the hook as possible and wind the yarn over the hook, placing the hook at the far side of the bead.

3 Now draw the yarn through both the loops on the hook to complete the stitch, keeping the bead at the front of the work. This method ensures that the bead stays firmly in place and does not slip through to the back of the work once the crochet has been completed.

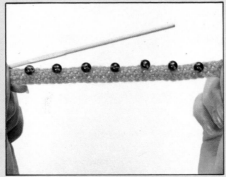

4 Continue to work a bead on every following 4th stitch in the same way, working the last single crochet into the top of the turning chain. The beads can be worked more closely if necessary, but when working with large beads keep one stitch between each bead.

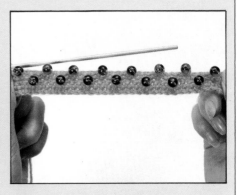

5 Turn and work 1 single crochet row. Now alternate the position of the beads on the next row by working the first bead with the 2nd stitch and then every following 4th stitch as before.

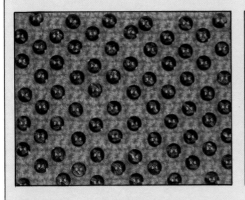

6 This sample shows several rows of beads with positions alternated on every bead row to create this simple pattern. Work a single crochet row between each bead row.

7 To work a bead with the wrong side of the work facing, work to the position for the bead. Insert the hook into the next stitch and draw through a loop in the usual way. Push the bead up close to the hook and wind the yarn over the hook at the far side of the bead.

8 Complete the stitch by drawing the yarn through the 2 loops on the hook. This sample shows beads worked on every row. One bead has been worked into every other stitch on the first (right side) row and the position of the beads alternated on the 2nd (wrong side) row to form this beaded fabric.

Working half doubles with beads

1 On the right side of the fabric work to the position for the bead. Wind the yarn over the hook and insert the hook from back to front through the next stitch. Wind yarn over the hook and draw it through so that yarn is at front.

2 Push the bead up close to the hook, wind the yarn over the hook at the far side of the bead and draw the yarn through the 3 loops on the hook to complete the stitch.

3 When working on the wrong side of the fabric wind the yarn over the hook and insert it into the next stitch. Draw a loop through in the normal way.

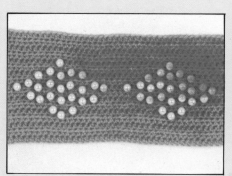

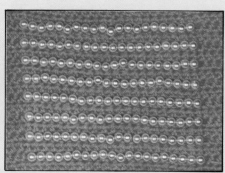

4 Push the bead up close to the hook, wind the yarn over the hook just beyond the bead and draw the yarn through all 3 loops on the hook to complete the stitch.

5 These diamonds have been worked by starting with 1 bead worked on the right side of the half double fabric. Beads are then worked on every row, working 3 half doubles between each bead until five beads have been worked in all. Shape the other side by working back in the same way until there is one bead at the center. Use the diamonds as an edging for an evening top or skirt.

6 In this sample beads have been worked on the right side of the work only, working a bead into consecutive stitches across the row.

Working doubles with beads

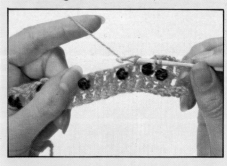

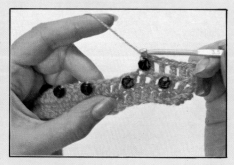

1 To work a beaded double on the right side of the work, wind the yarn over the hook, slip the bead up close to the hook and insert the hook into the next stitch, taking the hook over the working yarn so that bead is held at front of work.

2 Wind yarn over hook and draw through a loop. Wind yarn over hook and draw through first 2 loops. Now wind yarn over hook and draw it through last 2 loops to complete the double in the normal way.

3 To work a beaded double on the wrong side, wind yarn over hook and insert hook into next stitch. Wind yarn over hook and draw through a loop. Now wind yarn over hook and draw through first 2 loops on hook. 2 loops remain.

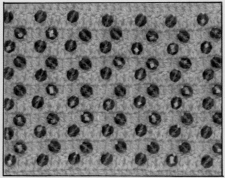

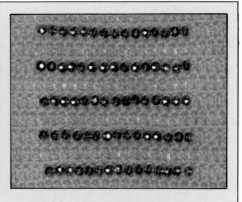

4 Slip the bead up close to the hook on the right side of the work. Wind the yarn over the hook just beyond the bead.

5 Now draw the yarn on the hook through the remaining 2 loops to complete the stitch. Here beads have been worked on the right and wrong side of a double crochet fabric. Beads worked on the right side lie at the bottom of the stitch, whereas those worked on the wrong side lie at the top of the stitch.

6 In this sample the beads have been worked on the wrong side of the work on every alternate (wrong side) row, so that the beads lie at the top of the stitch each time.

Stitch Wise

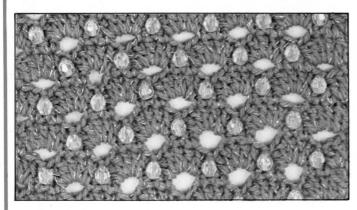

Beaded shell pattern

Make a multiple of 6 chains plus 3 for this pattern.
1st row (WS) 1sc into 3rd ch from hook, 1sc into next ch, *3ch, skip 3ch, 1sc into each of next 3ch, rep from *, ending last rep with 3ch, skip 3ch, 1sc into each of last 2ch. Turn.
2nd row 1ch, skip first sc, 1sc into next sc, *5dc into next 3ch space—called shell—, skip 1sc, work 1 bead into next sc (see step-by-step instructions page 1375)—called B1—, skip next sc, rep from *, ending last rep with skip 1sc, 1sc into turning chain. Turn.
3rd row 4ch to count as first sc and 3ch space, *1sc into each of 3 center dc of shell, 3ch, rep from *, ending with 2ch, 1sc into top of turning chain. Turn.
4th row 3ch to count as first dc, 2dc into first 2ch space, *skip 1sc, B1 into next sc, skip next sc, shell into next 3ch space, rep from * ending last rep with 3dc into space between last st and turning chain. Turn.

5th row 1ch, skip first st, 1sc into next st, *3ch, 1sc into each of 3 center dc of next shell, rep from *, ending with 1sc into last dc, 1sc into top of turning chain. Turn.
2nd to 5th rows form patt and are rep throughout.
To work patt without beads substitute B1 with 1sc.

Triangular bead pattern

Make a multiple of 8 chains plus 1, with 1 extra for turning chain.
1st row (RS) 1hdc into 3rd ch from hook, 1hdc into each ch to end. Turn.
2nd row 2ch, skip first hdc, 1hdc into each of next 2hdc, *(yo and insert hook into next st, yo and draw through a loop, push bead up to hook, yo beyond bead and draw yarn through 3 loops on hook—called bead 1 wrong side or, B1WS—,) 3 times, 1hdc into each of next 5 sts, rep from * to last 6 sts, B1WS into each of next 3 sts, 1hdc into each of next 2 sts, 1hdc into top of turning chain. Turn.

3rd row 2ch, skip first st, 1hdc into each of next 3 sts, *yo and insert hook from back to front into next st, yo and draw through a loop, slip bead up to hook, yo beyond bead and draw yarn through 3 loops on hook—called bead 1 right side (B1RS)—, work 1hdc into each of next 7 sts, rep from * to last 5 sts, B1RS into next st, 1hdc into each of next 3 sts, 1dc into turning chain. Turn.
4th row 2ch, skip first st, 1hdc into each st to end, working last dc into turning chain. Turn.
5th row As 4th.
6th row 2ch, skip first st, 1hdc into each of next 6 sts, *(B1WS into next st) 3 times, 1hdc into each of next 5 sts, rep from * to last 2 sts, 1hdc into next st, 1hdc into top of turning chain. Turn.
7th row 2ch, skip first st, *1hdc into each of next 7 sts, B1RS into next st, rep from * to last 8 sts, 1hdc into each st to end, 1hdc into turning chain. Turn.
8th-9th rows As 4th row.
The 2nd to 9th rows form patt and are rep throughout.

Beaded sweater

Worked in a soft yarn with pearl beads, this sweater is comfortable and glamorous.

Sizes
To fit 32-34[36-38]in (83-87[92-97]cm) bust. Length, 26½[27]in (66.5[67]cm). Sleeve, 17½in (44cm).
Note: Directions for larger size are in brackets []; if there is only one set of figures it applies to both sizes.

Materials
13[15]oz (360[400]g) of a fluffy sport-weight yarn
Size G (4.50mm) crochet hook
696[724] × ¼in (6mm) beads

Gauge
17 sts and 12 rows to 4in (10cm) worked on size G (4.50mm) hook.

Back
Using size G (4.50mm) hook make 82[90]ch.
Base row 1hdc into 3rd ch from hook, 1hdc into each of next 2ch, *1ch, skip next ch, 1hdc into each of next 7ch, rep from * to within last 5ch, 1ch, skip next ch, 1hdc into each of last 4ch. Turn. 81[89] sts. ** Beg patt.
1st row (RS) 2ch to count as first hdc, 1hdc into next hdc, *2ch, skip next 2hdc, 1sc into next sp, 2ch, skip next 2hdc, 1hdc into each of next 3hdc, rep from * to within last 7 sts, 2ch, skip next 2hdc, 1sc into next sp, 2ch, skip next 2hdc, 1hdc into each of last 2 sts. Fasten off and turn.
2nd row Thread 9[10] beads onto yarn, rejoin yarn to beg of row, 2ch, 1hdc into next hdc, *1hdc into next sp, 2ch, skip next sc, 1hdc into next sp, 1hdc into each of next 3hdc setting in one bead at the back of work on center of these 3 hdc, rep from *, finishing last rep 1hdc into each of last sts (not setting in a bead). Turn.
3rd row 2ch, 1hdc into each of next 2hdc, *1hdc into next sp, 1ch, 1hdc into same sp, 1hdc into each of next 5 hdc, rep from * finishing last rep 1hdc into each of last 3hdc. Turn.
4th row 2ch, *1hdc into each of next 3 hdc, 1hdc into next sp, 1hdc into each of next 3hdc, 1ch, skip next hdc, rep from *, omitting 1ch at end of last rep, 1hdc into top of 2ch. Turn.
5th row 1ch, 1sc into first hdc, *2ch, skip next 2hdc, 1hdc into each of next 3hdc, 2ch, skip next 2hdc, 1sc into next sp, rep from * working last 1sc into top of 2ch. Fasten off and turn.
6th row Thread 10[11] beads onto yarn and rejoin yarn to beg of row, 3ch to count as first hdc and sp, *1hdc into next sp, 1hdc into each of next 3hdc setting in

BACK

SLEEVE

SLEEVE

15¼ in

9[9½]in

17½ in

9[9½]in

FRONT

17½ in

19[21]in

Simon Butcher

one bead at the back of work on center of these 3hdc, 1hdc into next sp, 2ch, skip next sc, rep from * finishing last rep 1hdc into last sp, 1ch, 1hdc into last sc. Turn.
7th row 2ch, 1hdc into next sp, *1hdc into each of next 5hdc, 1hdc into next sp, 1ch, 1hdc into same sp, rep from * working last rep 1hdc into each of last 7 sts. Turn.
8th row 2ch, *1hdc into each of next 3hdc, 1ch, skip next hdc, 1hdc into each of next 3hdc, 1hdc into next sp, rep from * working last hdc into top of 2ch. Turn.
These 8 rows form the patt. Rep them 5 times more, then work rows 1 to 4 again. (53 rows have been worked from beg.)**

Shape raglan armholes
Next row Sl st across first 4hdc, 2ch, 1hdc into each of next 2hdc, patt to within last 3 sts. Fasten off and turn. 75[83] sts.
Next row Thread 8[9] beads onto yarn, rejoin yarn to 2nd hdc, 2ch, patt to within last st. Turn.
Keeping patt correct, work 25[26] more rows setting in 7[8] beads on next bead row and 6[7] beads on foll bead row and dec one st at each end of every row. 23[29] sts.
Fasten off.

Front
Work as for back until front measures 9[10] rows less than back.

Divide for opening
Next row Dec one st, patt as for 7th row ending with 2hdc into sp at center [for first size 1hdc into 3rd of 5hdc at center], for 2nd size turn and cont to shape raglan only, work until 27[28] rows have been completed from beg of raglan shaping. Fasten off.
With RS facing join yarn to same place as last st worked on first side, complete to match first side reversing shaping.

Sleeves
Using size G (4.50mm) hook make 66ch and work base row as for back. 65 sts.
Now work as for back from ** to ** setting in 7 and 8 beads alternately.
Shape raglan armhole
Work as back raglan, setting in 6, 5 and 4 beads respectively, until 7[5] sts rem. Fasten off.

Collar
Using size G (4.50mm) hook make 65ch.
1st row 1sc into 6th ch from hook, *3ch, 1sc into next ch, rep from * to end. Turn. 60 loops.
2nd row 4ch, 1sc into first loop, *3ch, 1sc into next loop, rep from * to end. Turn.
Rep 2nd row 6 times more.
9th row 5ch, 1sc into first loop, *4ch, 1sc into next loop, rep from * to end. Turn.

Rep 9th row 5 times more.
Fasten off and turn.
15th row Thread 60 beads onto yarn, rejoin yarn at beg of row, work as for 9th row setting in one bead at the back of work on each sc. Fasten off and turn.
16th row Work as for 15th row but set in beads at front of work on each sc.
17th row As 15th.

To finish
Do not press. Join raglan armholes, then join side and sleeve seams. Join foundation ch of collar to neck edge by working a row of sc through the double thickness, do not fasten off but turn and work eyelet hole row thus: 3ch, skip first sc, 1hdc into next sc, *1ch, skip next sc, 1hdc into next sc, rep from * to end. Fasten off.
With RS facing work a row of sc around lower edge of one sleeve. Do not fasten off but turn and work eyelet hole row as for neck. Finish other sleeve in the same way.

Ties
Using yarn double make a ch 30in (75cm) long for neck, 50in (130cm) long for waist and two 18in (45cm) long for sleeves. Thread ties through eyelet holes at neck and lower edge of sleeves and through patt at waist.

Crochet / COURSE 54

*Fine filet edgings
*Making a mitered corner
*Working filet blocks at a
 corner
*How to draw a corner
 on a chart
*Patterns for hanky edgings

Fine filet edgings

You can use all the basic filet crochet techniques learned so far to work fine filet edgings and borders. They make ideal trimmings for many household items including sheets, pillowcases and table-cloths. You could trim the edge of a collar or handkerchief with a narrow edging, or make a very deep, more intricately-pat-terned border with a serrated edge to sew around the edge of a bedspread or plain tablecloth.

The edgings can be worked lengthwise so that the number of foundation chains equals the total length of the edging, the **width** being determined by the number of rows worked. Or you can work the edgings widthwise so that the foundation chain is equal to the width, the **length** in this case being determined by the number of rows worked.

Both methods can be used where a straight strip is required, but when trim-ming a square or rectangular fabric, use the second method so that you can miter the corners while you work. This will ensure that the corners fit neatly and evenly around the fabric and that the con-tinuity of the pattern is maintained all the way around the edge.

In this course we show you how to work a mitered corner when working two simple filet patterns, but the same technique can be used for much more complicated filet patterns. For detailed directions for plain filet mesh patterns see Volume 7, pages 17 and 22. Instructions for work-ing from a chart are given in Volume 7, pages 24 and 25, and for increasing and decreasing in Volume 8, pages 4-7.

Making a mitered corner

Sooner or later you will want to trim the edge of a fabric where it will be necessary to work corners into your filet edging instead of working straight strips and sewing them separately onto the fabric. Here we show you the basic method for working a mitered corner. We have used a knitting worsted for this sample in two colors coded A and B, so that you can see exactly how the corner is worked. The sample has been made in the basic net pattern, in which 2 chains are worked between doubles, skipping 2 chains in the row below to form the spaces (see Volume 7, page 17).

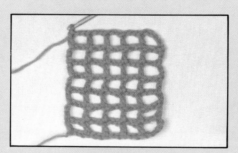

1 With A make 20 chains. 1 double into 8th chain from hook. 2 chains, skip 2 chains, 1 double into next chain. Repeat to end. Work 7 rows in pattern. Start each row with 5 chains and end 1 double into 3rd of 5 chains.

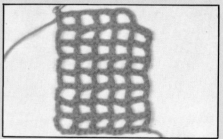

2 Now start to shape the corner. Skip the first stitch and work a slip stitch into each of the next 2 chains and into the next double to decrease the first space. Make 5 chains and then continue in pattern to the end of the row.

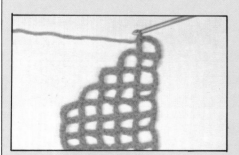

3 Turn and work back along the next row, leaving the last space unworked to decrease another space at the same side as before. Continue to decrease at the beginning or end of each row until one square remains.

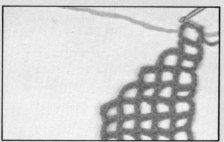

4 Now work one more row on this remaining square by working 5 chains and then a double into the 3rd of the 5 turning chains. Change to B while working the last double. Now turn and slip stitch across top of this square to inner edge.

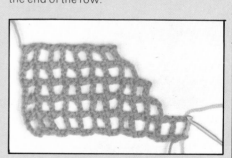

5 Now turn the work to the left so that the side edge becomes the lower edge; the lower edge is at the left-hand side of the work and the shaped edge along the top with the single square at the right-hand side.

Mike Berend

continued

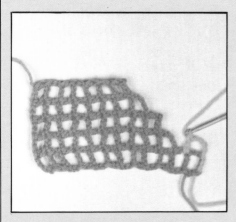

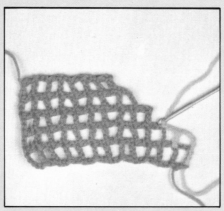

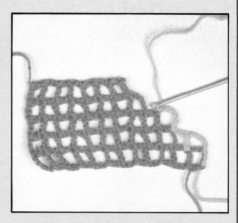

6 Make 5 chains to count as the first double and 2-chain space. Now work 1 double into the edge of the 2-chain bar to the left of the hook, between the last 2 spaces worked in A.

7 Make 2 chains, skip the inner corner between the next space and the next step worked in A, and work a slip stitch into the top right-hand corner of the next space worked in A, so that you are working into the 3rd of the 5 chains which form the side of this space.

8 Make 5 chains, skip the inner corner between the next space and the next step worked in A, and slip stitch into the top right-hand corner of the next space worked in A.

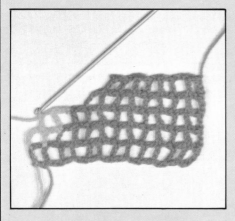

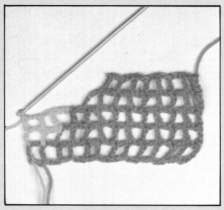

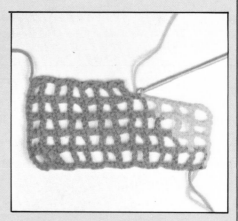

9 Now turn and continue to work back to the straight side edge again. Slip stitch across the first 2 chains in B, make 2 chains, and work a double into the next double worked in B.

10 Make 2 chains and work a double into the 3rd of the first 5 chains worked in B at the edge of the work.

11 Turn and work in the basic filet pattern as before over the first 3 spaces in B. Now make 2 chains and work a slip stitch into the 3rd of the next 5 chains worked in A.

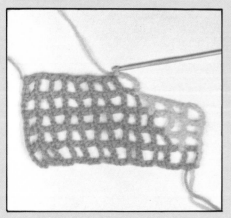

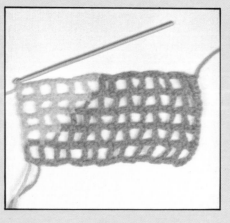

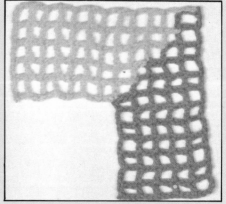

12 Make 5 chains and slip stitch into the top right-hand corner of the next space worked in A, as before.

13 Now turn, slip stitch across the first 2 chains in B, (2 chains, 1 double into next double in B) 3 times, 2 chains, 1 double into the 3rd of the 5 chains in B.

14 Now complete the edging by working in the basic filet pattern on the B side of the edging only. Note the line of triangular-shaped spaces at the 45° angle where the corner has been worked.

Working filet blocks at a corner

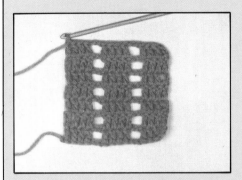

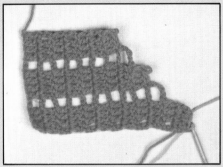

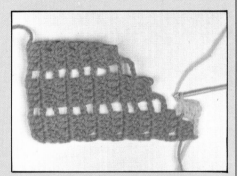

1 Use the same basic technique as when working the plain filet mesh. Here we have made a sample with 5 squares as before, but working a block and space alternately across 19 foundation chains. Work 2 doubles into the spaces to form the blocks so that each block consists of 4 doubles in all.

2 Shape the corner in the same way as when working the mesh shaping. Slip stitch across the top of a block or space to be decreased at the beginning of a row or leave a block or space unworked at the end of the row until one block remains. Then work 1 more block as shown here. We have changed colors for clarity.

3 Slip stitch across the top of the last block and turn the work so that the shaped edge is at the top. Make 3 chains to count as the first double and work 2 doubles into the side of the first block and 1 double into the top of double of the 2nd block worked previously in A to make the first block in B.

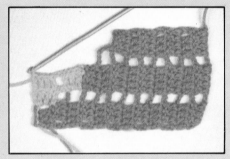

4 Make 2 chains and work a slip stitch into the 3rd of the next 5 chains worked in A. Make 3 chains and work 2 doubles into the side of the next space worked in A. Now slip stitch into the top right-hand corner of the next block worked in A. The top edge of the block worked in A counts as the 4th double of the block worked in B.

5 Now turn and slip stitch across the top of the block just worked, make 2 chains and work 1 double into the next double worked in B.

6 Now work 1 double into each of the next 2 doubles and complete the row by working 1 double into top of the first 3 chains at the edge of the work.

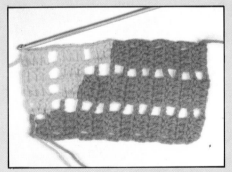

7 Turn. Work 1 block, 1 space and 1 block, working last double of the last block into the corner of the next block worked in A. Now make 2 chains and slip stitch into the 3rd of the next 5 chains worked in A.

8 Make 3 chains and work 2 doubles into the side of the next space worked in A, slip stitch into the top right-hand corner of next block worked in A as before. Turn, slip stitch across first block worked in B and complete the row with (1 space, 1 block) twice, ending at side edge.

9 Continue to work in the block and space pattern as now set so that you work only across the squares worked in B to complete the edging, noting that on the first row the last double of the last block is worked into the corner where A and B join. You will see that the blocks and spaces maintain the correct position on each side of the corner.

Terry Evans

Mike Berend

How to draw a corner on a chart

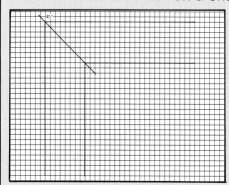

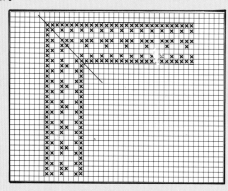

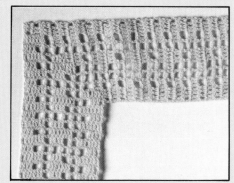

1 Draw the pattern on graph paper as described in Volume 7, page 22, so that each space and block in your pattern is represented by a blank square or an X on the paper. Read the graph from the bottom right-hand corner, reading right side rows from right to left and wrong side rows from left to right. Draw the shape of the edging on the paper, then draw a line through the corner at a 45° angle as shown here.

2 Now draw your pattern on the graph paper in the usual way. Take the pattern up to the corner line and then "mirror" the pattern on the other side of the line, so that when the piece is folded on the corner line each stitch marked on one side of the line fits exactly over the corresponding stitch on the other side of the line.

3 This sample shows the pattern worked from the graph shown in step 2, using the same method for shaping the corner as shown in the step-by-step instructions on page 17. The sample has been worked in fine cotton thread for the best results.

Hanky edgings

Work a pretty filet edging to brighten a cotton hanky.

Materials

Use a No. 7 (1.50mm) steel crochet hook and one 1oz (20g) ball of fine mercerized crochet cotton for each hanky

Following key below, repeat pattern until edging fits one edge. Work mitered corner, working from chart up to bold line (so working one space or block less per row at inside edge) and at same time keeping pattern correct at outer edge. When one half of the corner has been worked turn chart. Work second half of corner.

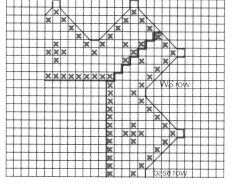

Beg with 20ch.
Base row 1dc into 8th ch from hook, 1dc into each of next 3ch, (2ch, skip next 2ch, 1dc into next ch) twice, 1dc into each of last 3ch. Turn.

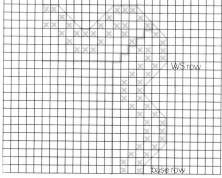

Beg with 15ch.
Base row 1dc into 4th ch from hook, 1dc into each of next 2ch, 2ch, skip next 2ch, 1dc into each of next 4ch, 2ch, skip next 2ch, 1dc into last dc. Turn.

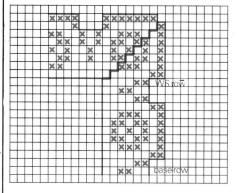

Beg with 23ch.
Base row 1dc into 8th ch from hook, 2ch, skip next 2ch, 1dc into each of next 7ch, (2ch, skip next 2ch, 1dc into next ch) twice. Turn.

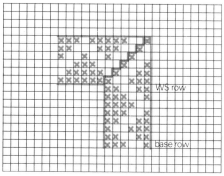

Beg with 21ch.
Base row 1dc into 4th ch from hook, 1dc into each of next 2ch, (2ch, skip next 2ch, 1dc into next ch) twice, 1dc into each of last 9ch. Turn.

KEY
□ = 1 space (1dc, 2ch and 1dc)
⊠ = 1 block (4dc plus 3 extra dc for each additional block)
▽ = inc at beg or end of row — at beg work 6ch, 1dc into next dc; at end work 2ch, 1tr into last st
◁ = dec at beg or end of row — at beg work 3ch, skip next 2 sts, 1dc into next dc, at end work skip next 2 sts, 1tr into next dc
□⊳ = picot — 5ch, sl st into 3rd ch from hook, 2ch, 1dc into next dc
 □ = inc 1 space — 5ch, 1dc into first st
⊠ = inc 1 block — 5ch, 1dc into 4th ch from hook, 1dc into next ch, 1dc into next dc
⊠⊠ = inc 2 blocks — 8ch, 1dc into 4th ch from hook, then 1dc into each ch

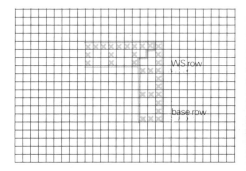

Beg with 12ch.
Base row 1dc into 4th ch from hook, 1dc into each ch to end. Turn.

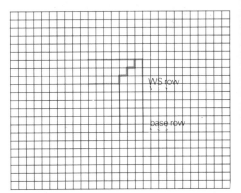

Beg with 14ch.
Base row 1dc into 8th ch from hook, (2ch, skip next 2ch, 1dc into next ch) twice. Turn.

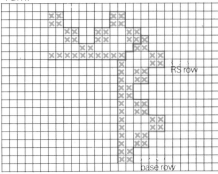

Beg with 9ch.
Base row 1dc into 4th ch from hook, 1dc into each of last 5ch. Turn.

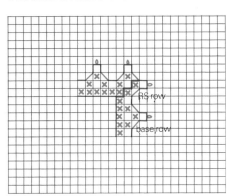

Beg with 11ch.
Base row 1dc into 8th ch from hook, 1dc into each of last 3ch. Turn.

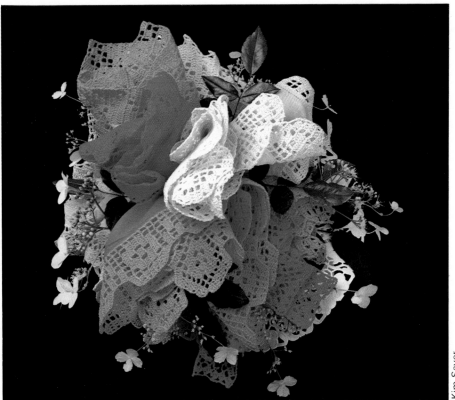

Kim Sayer

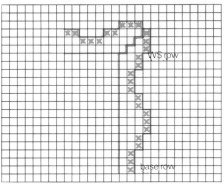

Beg with 9ch.
Base row 1dc into 4th ch from hook, 1dc into each of next 2ch, skip next 2ch, 1dc into last ch. Turn.

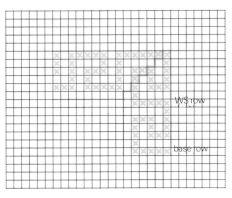

Beg with 21ch.
Base row 1dc into 4th ch from hook, 1dc into each of next 14ch, 2ch, skip next 2ch, 1dc into last ch. Turn.

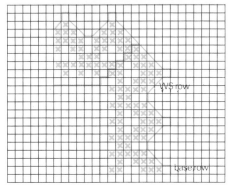

Beg with 32ch.
Base row 1dc into 8th ch from hook, 1dc into each of next 9ch, (2ch, skip next 2ch, 1dc into next ch) twice, 1dc into each of next 6ch, 2ch, skip next 2ch, 1dc into last ch. Turn.

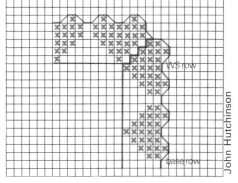

John Hutchinson

Beg with 20ch.
Base row 1dc into 8th ch from hook, (2ch, skip next 2ch, 1dc into next ch) 4 times. Turn.

You beautiful doll

Lengthen this skirt to make a pretty evening dress.

Size
To fit 11½in (29cm) fashion doll. Length of dress, 6in (15cm).

Materials
1oz (25g) of a sport yarn in each of 3 contrasting colors (A, B and C)
Nos. 3 and 9 (3¼ and 6mm) knitting needles
Size C (3mm) crochet hook

Gauge
20 sts and 24 rows to 4in (10cm) in stockinette st on No. 9 (6mm) needles. 14 sts and 23 rows to 2in (5cm) in seed st patt worked on No. 3 (3¼mm) needles.

Dress
Skirt
Using larger needles and A, cast on 60 sts. Change to B and beg by working in seed st patt as foll:
1st seed st row *K1, P1, rep from * to end.
2nd seed st row *P1, K1, rep from * to end.
Rep first and 2nd rows to form the seed st patt. Cont in seed st until work measures 1in (2.5cm) from beg. Change to C and work in stockinette st until work measures 2in (5cm) from beg. Then work in seed st until work measures 3in (7.5cm) from beg ending with a RS row.
Work 5 rows in stockinette st beg with a P row and ending with a P row.

Shape waist
Change to smaller needles and shape waist as foll:
Next row *P2tog, rep from * to end. 30 sts.
Next row *K1, P1, rep from * to end.
Rep last ribbing row 4 more times.

Top
Work top in seed st patt throughout. Work 9 rows. Bind off 7 sts in patt at beg of each of next 2 rows. 16 sts. Work shoulder straps and neck as foll:
Next row Work first 6 sts, turn leaving last 10 sts unworked.
Work one more row on these 6 sts.
Next row Work first 6 sts, pick up and work 2 sts at neck edge after 6th st, work next 10 sts. 18 sts.
Next row Work first 6 sts, turn leaving last 12 sts unworked.
Work one more row on these 6 sts.
Next row Work first 6 sts, pick up and work 2 sts at neck edge, work next 10sts. 20 sts.
Next row Work 6 sts, bind off next 8 sts in patt, work 6 sts.
Next row Work first 6 sts, turn leaving last 6 sts unworked. Work 13 more rows on

these 6 sts to form first shoulder strap. Bind off in patt. Join yarn to last 6 sts on needle. Work 14 rows in patt on these sts. Bind off in patt.

To finish
Press or block skirt only, according to yarn used. Sew back seam. Sew shoulder straps to back. Darn in loose ends.
To make belts: Using size C (3mm) crochet hook and B make a chain 15in (38cm) long. Belt can be threaded through waistband so that a child will not lose it. Put doll into dress feet first.

Handbag
Using size 9 (6mm) needles and C cast on 25 sts.
Work in seed st patt until work measures 1½in (4cm) from beg. Change to size 3 (3¼mm) needles and B and work 3 rows of K1, P1 ribbing. Using A bind off in ribbing.

To finish
Do not press. Fold piece in half sideways. Sew side and bottom seams. Darn in

loose ends. To make bag strap: using crochet hook and A, make a chain 2¾in (7cm) long. Sew strap to bag.

Hat
Using size 3 (3¼mm) needles and A cast on 50 sts.
Change to B and work 2 rows in seed st patt. P one row. K one row.
Next row * P2 tog, P1, rep from * to end. 33 sts.
K one row.
Next row *P2 tog, P1, rep from * to end. 22 sts. K one row. P one row.
Change to size 9 (6mm) needles and using C work in seed st for 6 rows.
Next row *P2 tog, rep from * to end. 11 sts. Cut yarn leaving a long loose end. Thread tapestry needle with long end of yarn and pass needle through rem 11 sts. Pull yarn to gather sts.

To finish
With RS tog sew back seam of hat. Darn in loose ends. Press or block brim only. Turn brim up or down as desired.

Ron Kelly

Crochet / COURSE 55

More filet crochet

In this course we show you how to work the V-shaped filet pattern, called a "lacet," which is frequently used in filet designs to create a lacy fabric.

The lacet can be used either along with, or in place of, a block or space in your pattern to produce lovely fabrics ideal for many household items, including bedspreads, tablecloths, curtains and filet crochet edgings.

Although filet designs can be worked in any yarn, they are most successful when worked in a cotton yarn—fine or thick, depending on the article to be made—thus creating the crisp fabric associated with traditional filet crochet.

There are many different cotton yarns on the market today, available in a wide range of colors, so you should have no difficulty in finding a yarn to suit your design, whether you are looking for a very fine crochet cotton for a lacy edging, or something much heavier for a filet crochet bedspread.

Lacet patterns

A lacet is worked over two rows in a filet crochet pattern, so that the V-shaped group is worked on the first row, followed by a 5-chain bar worked on the following row. This should be taken into account when working out your own filet design on graph paper (see Volume 7, page 25). Allow 2 rows each time for any lacet worked in the pattern, whether you intend to work only one at the centre of a motif, for example, or several across the width of the fabric.

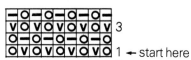

3
1 ← start here

O = block (5 doubles)
V = lacet (3ch, 1sc, 3ch)
— = 5-chain bar

1 This chart shows a simple block and lacet pattern worked out on graph paper. The lacet is shown as a V on the graph, with the 5-chain bar shown as a — over the top of the V group. Read the chart from the bottom right-hand corner in the normal way. Blocks have been shown as an O on this chart for clarity.

2 Make 47 chains for a sample like the one shown here. Now work the first block, which should consist of 5 doubles in all, working the first double into the 4th chain from the hook. You must work an uneven number of stitches in each block so that the V can be worked into the center stitch on following rows.

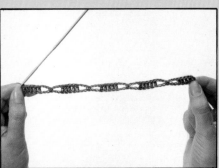

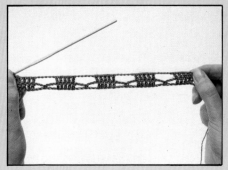

3 Now work the first lacet by making 3 chains, skip the next 2 chains, work a single crochet into the next chain, make 3 chains, skip the next 2 chains and work a double into the next chain.

4 Continue to work alternate blocks and lacets along the foundation chain in this way, remembering that the last double of each lacet is also counted as the first double of the next block.

5 To complete the two lacet rows, work a block over each block and a 5-chain bar over each lacet worked in the previous row. Start with 3 chains and work the last double into the top of the turning chain.

Mike Berend

continued

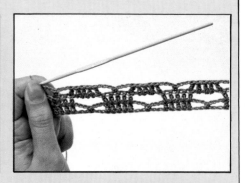

6 To continue the pattern from the chart, begin the next row with 6 chains (3 for the first double and 3 for the first part of the V). Work a single crochet into the center double of the first block, make 3 chains, and work a double into last double of the same block to complete the lacet.

7 Now work 3 doubles into the next 5-chain space, followed by a double into the next double to make a block consisting of 5 doubles in all.

8 Continue to work a block over each lacet and a lacet over each block to the end of the row, working the last double into the turning chain.

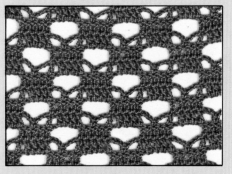

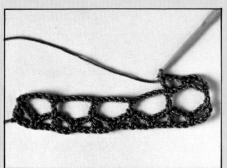

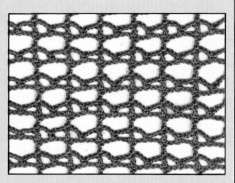

9 Here we show a completed sample worked from the chart, so that the blocks and lacets change position after two rows each time.

10 To work a lacet over a lacet, work the single crochet into the 3rd of the 5 chains worked in the previous row as shown here. Note that the double which completes the lacet is worked into the first double of the next lacet.

11 This sample shows lacet worked as an allover pattern. In this case the single crochet is worked into the center of the 5-chain bar each time to create the V, with a double worked into each double worked in the previous row.

Filet squares

A simple but effective way of making a filet fabric is to work the patterns in squares rather than in one piece, so that the squares can be sewn together to form a complete fabric. This is an ideal way of making a large item like a bedspread or large cotton tablecloth, since the squares are much more convenient to handle than an enormous piece of crochet.

With careful planning and the use of all the different filet techniques, you can make many interesting patterns by working in this way. The stitches or blocks and spaces worked along the edges of your square can be worked so that they form a secondary pattern in the fabric when the squares are sewn together.

O = block (5 doubles)
V = lacet (3ch, 1sc, 3ch)
— = 5-chain bar

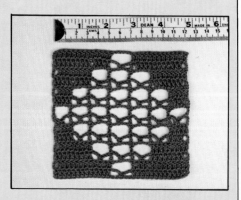

1 Plan your square on a graph. You can either make your own grid (see Volume 7, page 25) or use graph paper. Mark each block, space or lacet with a different symbol. Our graph uses an O for each block so that it stands out clearly against the V used to represent each lacet and the —for each 5-chain bar.

2 To calculate the number of squares needed, work a sample square in the yarn and hook of your choice. Pin it out so that it is square and press with a warm iron over a damp cloth. The sides of this square measure $4\frac{3}{4}$in (12cm). Make 80 for a rug 38 × $47\frac{1}{2}$in (96 × 120cm).

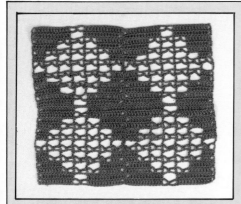

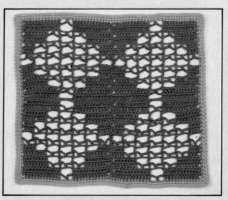

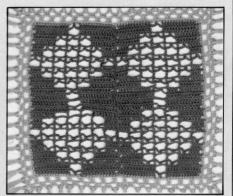

3 Four squares have been worked and sewn together using an invisible seam and matching thread. You can see that the blocks worked in a triangle on the corner of each square form a solid diamond shape when joined together, so that the completed fabric will consist of alternate open and solid diamond shapes.

4 Once you have worked all the squares and sewn them together, you should work an edging all the way around the fabric to ensure that your design has a firm, even edge. You can work a simple single crochet edging all the way around, working the number of rows needed for the width of the edging.

5 Or finish by working a simple space and block design as shown here, knotting a fringe into the spaces all the way around to complete the edging.

Mike Berend

Stitch Wise

Edgings

These two edgings can be worked either in a very fine or a medium-weight crochet cotton. Work the edgings from the charts, starting at the bottom right-hand corner and working every RS row from right to left and every WS row from left to right. They are both worked from side to side, so that you can make them any length you like.

Rose motif border

Make 21 chains.
1st row (RS) 1dc into 4th ch from hook, 1dc into each of next 2ch, (skip 2ch, 1dc into next ch) 4 times in all, 1dc into each of next 3dc. Turn. Now continue to work from chart so that the next (2nd) row of chart is worked from left to right. The pattern repeated is shown in parentheses and should be repeated for the length of the edging.
X =1 block (4 doubles)
☐ =1 space (1 double, 2 chains, 1 double)

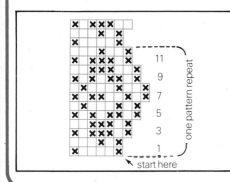

Border with looped edging

Make 45 chains.
Base row (WS) Work 1dc into 4th ch from hook, 1dc into each ch to end. Turn. Now continue to read the pattern from the chart, starting at 1st row of chart and noting that 1 pattern repeat has been shown between parentheses and should be repeated for the length of the edging.
X =1 block (4 doubles)
☐ =1 space (1 double, 2 chains, 1 double)

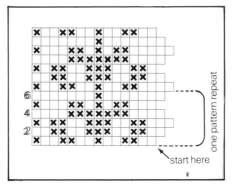

Allover patterns

Use these patterns for a complete filet crochet fabric. Follow the charts in the normal way, reading the right-side rows from right to left and wrong-side rows from left to right, starting at the bottom right-hand corner each time.

Diamond pattern

X =1 block (4 doubles)
☐ =1 space (1 double, 2 chains, 1 double)

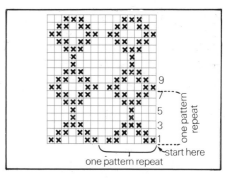

Lattice diamond pattern

X =1 block consisting of 5 doubles in all.
☐ =1 space (1 double, 3 chains, 1 double)
V =Lacet (3 chains, 1 single crochet, 3 chains)
— =5-chain bar over V in previous row.

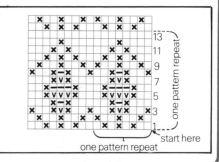

John Hutchinson

Cross-over filet blouse

Crochet this delicate evening top to express your most romantic mood.

Sizes

To fit 32[34:36]in (83[87:92]cm) bust. Length, 17[17½:18]in (44[45-46]cm) excluding edging.

Note Directions for larger sizes are in brackets []; where there is only one set of figures it applies to all sizes.

Materials

11[13:15]oz (300[350:400]g) of a lightweight mercerized crochet cotton
No. 0 (2.00mm) crochet hook
2 buttons

Gauge

30 sts and 18 rows to 4in (10cm) in pattern on No. 0 (2.00mm) hook.

Back

Using No. 0 (2.00mm) hook make 129[141:153]ch.
Base row *1dc into 4th ch from hook, 1dc into each ch to end. Turn. 127[139:151] sts.
1st row (WS) 3ch to count as first dc, 1dc into each of next 6dc, *3ch, skip next 2dc, 1sc into next dc, 3ch, skip next 2dc, 1dc into each of next 7dc, rep from * to end.
Turn.
2nd row 1ch to count as first sc, 1sc into each of next 6dc, *5ch, 1sc into each of next 7dc, rep from * to end.
3rd row 6ch, to count as first dc and 3ch, skip next 2sc, 1sc into next sc, 3ch, skip next 2sc, 1dc into next sc, *5dc into 5ch loop, 1dc into next sc, 3ch, skip next 2sc, 1sc into next sc, 3ch, skip next 2sc, 1dc into next sc, rep from * to end, working last dc into turning ch.
4th row 6ch, *1sc into each of next 7dc, 5ch, rep from * to end, 1sc into 3rd of 6ch.
5th row 3ch, *5dc into 5ch loop, 1dc into next sc, 3ch, skip next 2sc, 1sc into next sc, 3ch, skip next 2sc, 1dc into next sc, rep from * to last 5ch loop, 5dc into 5ch loop, 1dc into first of 6ch.
2nd-5th rows form patt. Cont in patt until work measures 17[17½:18]in (44[45:46]cm); end with a WS row.
Shape shoulder
Next row Sl st over first 10 sts, patt to within last 9 sts, turn.
Rep this row 3 times more.
Next row Sl st over first 5[8:11] sts, patt to within last 4[7:10] sts. Fasten off.

Left front

Using No. 0 (2.00mm) hook make 129[141:153]ch. Work base row and first 5 patt rows as given for back. **
Shape front edge
1st row Work as 2nd patt row, but ending with 1sc into each of next 4dc, turn.
2nd row 3ch, skip next 2sc, 1dc into next sc, work in patt to end as given for 3rd patt row.
Rep these 2 rows 6 times more. 88[100:112] sts.

Next row Patt to end as 2nd patt row ending with 7sc. Turn.
Work 3rd and 4th patt rows.
Next row Sl st over first 3ch, 3ch, 2dc into same sp, 1dc into next sc, patt to end. Turn.
Next 2 rows As 1st and 2nd shaping rows. Turn. 82[94:106] sts counting from first dc at beg of row.
Rep last 6 rows until 40[43:46] sts rem, then cont straight until work measures same as back to shoulders; end at side edge. Shape shoulder to match back.

Right front

Work as given for left front to **.
Next row Sl st over first 4dc, 1ch, 1sc into each of next 3dc, patt to end. Turn.
Next row Patt to end, ending with 5dc into 5ch loop, 1dc into next sc, 3ch, skip next 2sc, 1sc into next sc. Turn.
Next row Sl st over first 3ch, patt to end. Cont to match left front, reversing shaping.

Edging

Make 16ch.
1st row 1dc into 8th ch from hook, 3ch, skip next 2ch, 1sc into next ch, 3ch, skip next 2ch, 1dc into each of next 3ch. Turn.
2nd row 1ch, 1sc into each of next 2dc, 5ch, 1sc into next dc, 5ch, 1dc into 3rd of 7ch at beg of last row. Turn.
3rd row 9ch, 1dc into 3rd of 5ch, 3ch, 1dc into next sc, 3ch, 1sc into 3rd of 5ch, 3ch, 1dc into each of next 2sc, 1dc into turning ch. Turn.
4th row 1ch, 1sc into each of next 2dc, 5ch, 1sc, into next dc, 3ch, 1dc into 3rd of 9 turning ch. Turn.
5th row 3ch, 1dc into next sc, 3ch, 1sc into 3rd of 5ch, 3ch, 1dc into each of next 2sc, 1dc into turning ch. Turn.
6th row 1ch, 1sc into each of next 2dc, 5ch, 1dc into next dc. Turn.
7th row 7ch, 1dc into next sc, 3ch, 1sc into 3rd of 5ch, 3ch, 1dc into each of next 2sc, 1dc into turning ch. Turn.
Rep 2nd-7th rows until border measures 20½in (52cm); end with a 5th row. Fasten off. Make another piece in same way. Make 1 piece approx 33[36:39]in (84[92:100]cm) long.

To finish

Press work on WS with a warm iron over a damp cloth. Join shoulder seams. Sew two shorter pieces of edging to armholes. Join rem part of side seams. Sew longer piece of edging along lower edge of right front and back, ending at left side seam. With RS facing, work a row of sc up right front edge, around back neck and down left front, turn.
Next row *3ch, skip 1sc, 1sc into next sc, rep from * to end. Fasten off.
Sew one button to left side seam and make loop on right front edge. Sew a second button to inside of right side seam and make loop on left front edge.

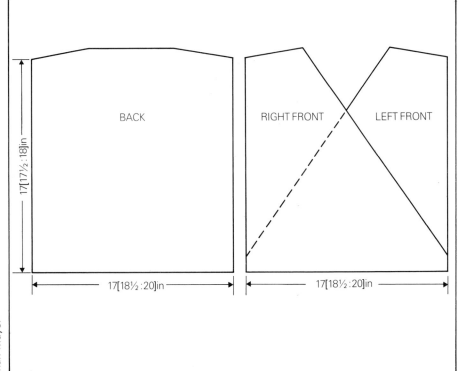

BACK

17[17½:18]in

17[18½:20]in

RIGHT FRONT

LEFT FRONT

17[18½:20]in

Crochet / COURSE 56

Aran-style patterns with surface crochet

We have already shown you how to work some of the background crochet patterns which produce an Aran-style fabric of crochet seed stitch, berry stitch or Aran ribbing patterns (see Volume 5, page 10) This course shows how to work crochet on the surface of the fabric after the basic shape has been completed, to create raised lines which can be shaped to form cables, diamonds or zig-zag patterns, or can be used to divide the fabric into separate panels to produce a heavily textured fabric, similar in appearance to the traditional patterns associated with Aran knitting.

The different shapes are formed by working up the fabric from the lower edge to the top edge, forming one side of the diamond, cable or zig-zag, then returning to the lower edge and working the other side to complete the shape. When you are working cables, you may have to cross one line of surface crochet over the top of the first line to achieve the best shape. There is an element of trial and error involved in forming these different shapes. For this reason, first make a sample using the yarn and hook of your choice, so that you can see exactly how the different shapes should be formed, before you start a garment.

Raised single crochet

Make a square of single crochet using a knitting worsted or thicker ply for the sample. We have used an Aran-style yarn and a size H (5.00mm) hook to make a firm fabric, using the same yarn in a contrasting color for the raised crochet, so that you can see exactly how the stitches are worked. For the most effective use of this technique you should use the same color for the background fabric and the raised or surface crochet when making a garment.

1 To introduce the yarn at the bottom of the fabric, hold the yarn at the back (wrong side) of the work and insert the hook into the foundation chain. Draw a loop through to the front of the work.

2 Now insert the hook into the next chain at the base of the work and draw another loop of yarn through to the front so that there are two loops on the hook. By working into two consecutive chains at the base you hold the yarn firmly in place.

3 Now insert the hook into the next row, immediately above the first loop, and draw through a loop. Now draw this loop through the first 2 loops on the hook to complete the first raised single crochet.

4 To continue working up the fabric, insert the hook into the **same** place as the last insertion and draw through a loop of yarn so that there are two loops on the hook.

5 Now insert the hook into the next row, immediately above the last stitch, and draw through a loop. Now draw this loop through the first two loops on the hook to complete the stitch as before.

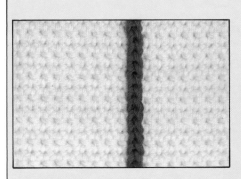

6 Continue to work a raised single crochet into each row in the same way. You will find that as the spaces do not lie immediately above each other in every row the hook will be placed either slightly to the right or slightly to the left each time, but the overall effect will still be a straight line once the crochet has been completed.

7 Here two sets of double lines have been worked at each side of a single crochet Aran ribbing pattern, thus dividing the work into panels. Leave one stitch between the lines of raised single crochet, worked from the bottom to the top edge each time, so that they stand out clearly against the background fabric.

8 To move the stitches to the right, work in exactly the same way as before, but complete each raised single crochet by inserting the hook one stitch to the right, one row above the last stitch each time.

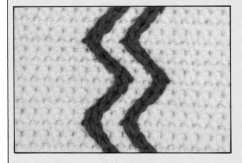

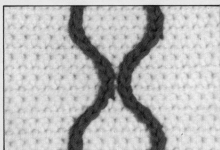

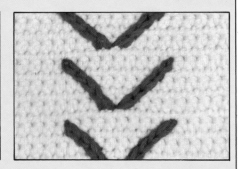

9 To move the stitches to the left, move the hook one stitch to the left and insert it into the row above the last stitch each time. This sample shows a double row of zig-zag lines worked on single crochet background fabric.

10 To curve the lines more gently, work one or more stitches in a straight line, depending on the shape desired, before turning the raised stitches to the right or left each time.

11 To introduce the yarn into the middle of the fabric, when working a broken cable or V-shaped pattern for example, insert the hook into the fabric between two stitches; then into the fabric to the left of this stitch, to secure the yarn before proceeding to work the raised stitches as before.

Raised single crochet on half double or double fabric

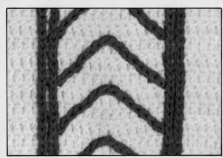

1 To work a raised single crochet on a half double fabric, use the same method as when working on a single crochet fabric, but if you find that the stitches are pulling the background fabric out of shape, work over half a row each time so that the first stitch is worked into the base of the first row.

2 The next stitch will then be worked into the middle of the same row and the next stitch into the base of the following row. Work alternately in this way either up or across the fabric so that you work into the base and then the middle of each row every time.

3 When working over a double fabric, use the same method so that you work into the middle of the first row, then the base of the next row. Continue working into the base then the middle of each double row, making sure that each stitch covers the fabric completely without pulling it out of shape.

Working crochet ribbing

The simplest method of creating a ribbed effect in crochet is to work into the back loops only of either single crochet or half double stitches. In this case the ribbing is worked as a separate piece from top to bottom, so that the number of stitches in each row is equivalent to the depth of the ribbing, the length being determined by the number of rows worked. Once the ribbing has been completed the crochet is turned and stitches are worked along the length of the ribbing to start the main part of the garment. If necessary, stitches can be increased across the row to make the fabric wider. For a bulkier ribbing, ideal for heavy pullovers and cardigans, a more textured effect can be achieved by working around the stem of either half doubles or doubles to form the ribbing. You will find that single crochet is too shallow to be effective when worked in this way.

1 Work the ribbing from side to side as usual. Start by making a number of chains equivalent to the length of ribbing required for your cuff or waistband. Then work 1 row half doubles in the normal way. Turn. Make 2 chains. Insert hook around stem of the 2nd half double worked in the previous row, inserting hook from front to back, then to the front again, to pull the stitch forward.

2 Continue to work around the stem of each stitch to the end of the row, working the last half double into the top of the turning chain so that all the stitches have been brought forward on the right side of the work.

3 On the next row work in half doubles, inserting the hook around the stem of each half double worked in the previous row, but placing the hook between the stitches from the back, around the front and then to the back again to hold them at the back or right side of the work. Alternate these two rows for the pattern.

4 Here several rows of ribbing form a neat cuff at the bottom of a sleeve. Stitches must be increased across the first row of the main part of the fabric for the width of the sleeve, since this ribbing does not expand in the normal way.

5 The back of the ribbing consists of a series of ribbed stitches lying horizontally across the crochet, forming a firm, double fabric.

6 Here doubles have been worked in exactly the same way, alternating the first, then the second, row each time to complete the pattern, so forming a wider ribbed effect.

7 To make a more elastic ribbing, which usually makes it unnecessary to increase stitches at the beginning of the main fabric, work the stitches around the stem in exactly the same way as before, but on the first row bring the first stitch to the front, then the second stitch to the back. Continue to alternate the stitches across the row in this way, working the last stitch into the top of the turning chain.

8 On the second row work around the stem of each stitch as before, keeping the ribbing pattern correct by working behind the stem of the stitches at the front of the fabric and around the front of the stitches at the back of the crochet each time to create the ribbed effect. Work in the same way on every row to complete the pattern whether working in half doubles or doubles.

Man's V-neck sweater

Bands of crochet ribbing at the cuffs and the waistband of this crochet sweater complement the main fabric, worked in doubles.

Sizes
To fit 40[42:44]in (102[107:112]cm) chest.
Length, 28[28½:29]in (71[72:73]cm).
Sleeve seam, 18in (46cm).
Note: Directions for larger sizes are in brackets []; if there is only one set of figures it applies to all sizes.

Materials
  39[41:43]oz (1100[1150:1200]g) of a knitting worsted
  Sizes F and G (4.00 and 4.50mm) crochet hooks

David Bradfield

John Hutchinson

Gauge
16dc and 8 rows to 4in (10cm) worked on size G (4.50mm) hook.

Back and front (alike)
Using size F (4.00mm) hook make 79[83:87]ch.
Base row 1hdc into 3rd ch from hook, 1hdc into each ch to end. Turn. 78[82:86]sts.
1st ribbing row 2ch to count as first hdc, *yo, insert hook from front to back between next 2hdc around hdc at left and through work from back to front, draw a loop through, yo and draw through all loops on hook–called 1hdc around front or 1hdc around Ft–, rep from * to end, 1hdc into top of turning ch. Turn.
2nd ribbing row *yo, insert hook from back to front between next 2hdc, around hdc at left and through work from front to back, draw a loop through, yo and draw through all loops on hook–called 1hdc around back or 1hdc around Bk–, rep from * to end, 1hdc into top of turning ch. Turn.
Rep last 2 rows until work measures $2\frac{3}{4}$in (7cm). Change to size G (4.50mm) hook.**
Inc row 3ch to count as first dc, 1dc into each of next 4hdc, (2dc into next hdc, 1dc into each of next 2hdc) 4 times, 1dc into each hdc until 15sts rem unworked, (2dc into next hdc, 1dc into each of next 2hdc) 4 times, 1dc into each of next 2hdc, 1dc into top of turning ch. Turn. 86[90:94]sts.
Patt row 3ch to count as first dc, 1dc into each dc to end. Turn.
Rep last row until 30dc rows in all have been worked and back measures $18\frac{1}{2}$in (47cm) from beg. Fasten off.

Back sleeve sections (make 2)
Using size F (4.00mm) hook make 19[21:23]ch. Work as for back to **. 18[20:22]sts. Beg patt.
1st row 3ch to count as first dc, 1dc into each hdc to end, 1dc into top of turning ch. Turn.
2nd row (inc) 3ch to count as first dc, 1dc into each of next 4dc, 2dc into next dc, 1dc into each dc to within last 6 sts, 2dc into next dc, 1dc into each dc to end, 1dc into turning ch. Turn. 20[22:24]sts.
3rd row 3ch to count as first dc, 1dc into each dc to end. Turn.
4th row As 3rd.
Rep 2nd-4th rows 9 times more. 38[40:42]sts.
Cont in patt without shaping until work measures $28\frac{3}{4}$[$29\frac{1}{4}$:$29\frac{3}{4}$]in (73[74:75.5]cm). Fasten off.

Front sleeve section
1st side Work as for back section until 10[11:12] rows less have been worked ***
Shape neck
1st size only
1st row Skip first dc, sl st into each of next 2dc, 3ch to count as first dc, 1dc into each dc to end. Turn.
2nd row 3ch, 1dc into each dc to within last 2sts, turn.
3rd row Skip first dc, sl st into each of next 4dc, 3ch, 1dc into each dc to end. Turn.
4th row 3ch, 1dc into each dc to within last 4sts, turn.
Rep 3rd and 4th rows until 2sts rem. Fasten off.
2nd size only
Work 1st and 2nd rows of 1st size, then work the 1st row again. Now work 4th and 3rd rows of 1st size until 2 sts rem. Fasten off.
3rd size only
Work 1st and 2nd rows of 1st size twice. Now work 3rd and 4th rows of 1st size until 2sts rem. Fasten off.
2nd size Work as given for 1st side to ***
Shape neck
1st size only
1st row 3ch, 1dc into each dc to within last 2 sts, turn.
2nd row Skip first dc, sl st into each of next 2dc, 3ch, 1dc into each dc to end, 1dc into top of turning ch. Turn.
3rd row 3ch, 1dc into each dc to within last 4sts, turn.
4th row Skip first dc, sl st into each of next 4dc, 3ch, 1dc into each dc to end, 1dc into top of turning ch. Turn.
Rep 3rd and 4th rows until 2 sts rem. Fasten off.
2nd size only
Work 1st and 2nd rows of 1st size, then work the 1st row again. Now work 4th and 3rd rows of 1st size, until 2 sts rem. Fasten off.
3rd size only
Work 1st and 2nd rows of 1st size twice, then work 3rd and 4th rows of 1st size until 2 sts rem. Fasten off.

Raised cable pattern
Using size G (4.50mm) hook work diamond patt on back and front working 2 vertical rows of diamonds 5 patts high, 1 vertical row 3 patts high and 2 vertical rows 5 patts high by working raised sc as in step-by-step instructions (see page 28), work 2 parallel rows of raised sc moving sts 6 spaces to right then 6 spaces to left to form patt. Place base of center diamond at center of fabric and base of adjacent patts 12 spaces from base of previous patts.

To finish
Join side, sleeve and center back seams. Join sleeve sections to top edge of back and front.
Neck edging
Using size F (4.00mm) hook and with RS facing, join yarn to right shoulder seam.
1st round 2ch, work in hdc evenly down side of neck to V, work 1hdc into center of V and mark st with a colored thread, work in hdc evenly up left side of neck and across back neck. Join with sl st to top of 2ch. Turn.
2nd round Work as for 2nd row of back waistband to within 1hdc of marked st, insert hook into each of next 3hdc and draw through a loop, yo and draw through all loops on hook (2hdc dec), cont as for 2nd row of back waistband to end of round. Join with a sl st to top of 2ch. Turn.
3rd round Work as for 1st row of back waistband to within 1hdc of marked st, dec 2hdc over next 3sts, cont in ribbing to end of round. Join with sl st to top of 2ch. Turn.
Rep 2nd round once more. Fasten off. Press seams lightly.

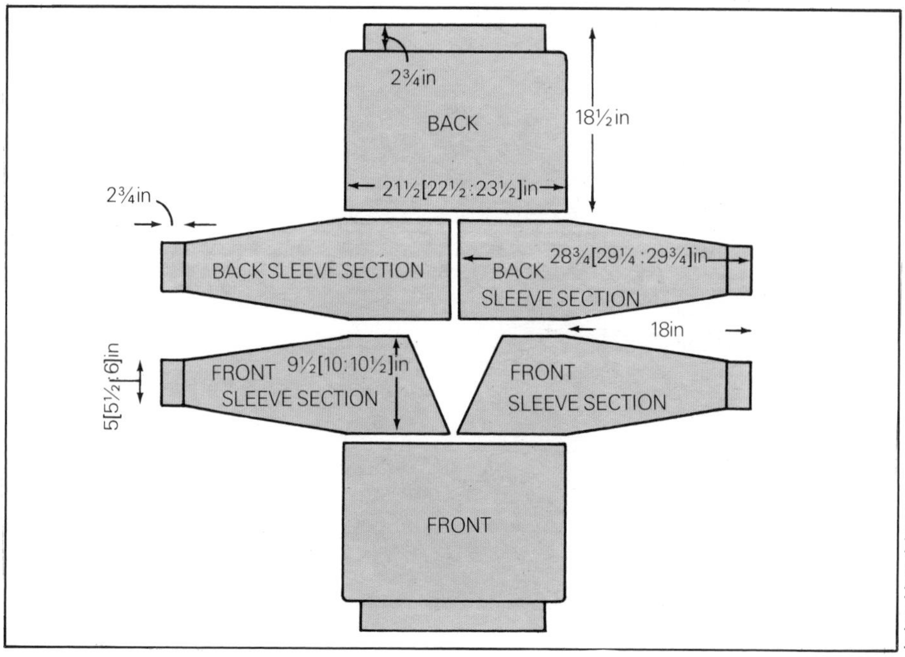
2¾in
BACK
18½in
21½[22½:23½]in
2¾in
BACK SLEEVE SECTION
BACK SLEEVE SECTION
28¾[29¼:29¾]in
18in
FRONT SLEEVE SECTION
9½[10:10½]in
5[5½:6]in
FRONT SLEEVE SECTION
FRONT

John Hutchinson

*Working horizontal tucks
*Working vertical tucks
*Pattern for a maternity
 dress and smock

Working horizontal tucks

Horizontal tucks are an easy-to-knit trimming that can be successfully incorporated into numerous garments; simply knit them into the fabric as you are working.

Tucks look particularly attractive in stockinette stitch, although you can use a number of variations, including the ones shown in the samples at the end of the step-by-step sequence.

Popular places to use tucks are on the hem of a skirt or dress, on a sleeve cuff or across the yoke of a sweater or dress. If you want to include tucks in a design, remember that you need more yarn than stated in the pattern; allow an extra ball or two.

1 Work in stockinette stitch to the position of the tuck, ending with a purl row. Tie a marker loop of different-colored yarn to the stitches at each end of the last row as shown here.

2 Depending on the depth of tuck you want, work a number of rows for the first side—here it is seven, ending with a knit row.

3 The edge of the tuck must be marked by a foldline so that it can be doubled neatly. Work the next row by knitting all the stitches through the back of the loops to produce a garter stitch ridge on the right side of the fabric.

4 Beginning with a knit row, work the second side of the tuck. Here there are six rows—one less than in the first side, so ending with a purl row.

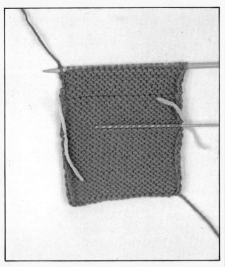

5 With the WS facing and using a spare needle, begin at the right-hand edge of the marked row and pick up the correct number of stitches along the row, inserting the needle from left to right under the top loop of each stitch. The points of both needles—that holding the stitches and the spare one—must be facing in the same direction.

continued

Mike Berend

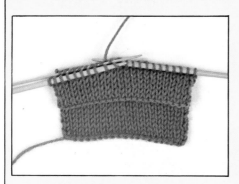

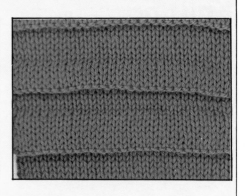

6 Knit the tuck in position. Hold the spare needle behind the one holding the stitches, but level with it. Knit to the end—of the row, working two stitches together—one from each of the needles—each time.

7 Beginning with a purl row, continue in stockinette stitch to the position of the next tuck. This is the finished tuck on the right side; the foldline makes a distinctive edge. The back of the fabric looks the same as it usually would.

8 You can vary the depth of tucks by varying the number of rows worked before folding the fabric in half. Here three, five and seven rows respectively have been worked in the first side of the tuck.

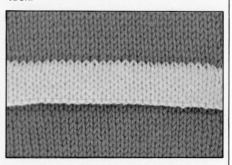

Make a pretty edging to a tuck by marking the foldline with a row or eyelet holes; these form a picot edge when the tuck is folded. After working the first side of the tuck, ending with a knit row, work the next row by knitting two stitches together and bringing the yarn over the needle to make a stitch.

Give tucks a distinctive texture by working them in reverse stockinette stitch. When you reach the position for the tuck, mark each end of the last (purl) row. Beginning with a purl row, work an uneven number of rows in reverse stockinette stitch. Mark the foldline by purling each stitch on the WS of the work. Continue in reverse stockinette stitch, reverting to normal stockinette stitch when you knit the tuck in position.

Tucks in a different color from the main fabric have a striking effect. When you join in the contrasting color at the beginning of a tuck, there is no need to cut off the main color. After working the tuck in the contrasting color, simply continue to use the main color from the point where you knit the tuck in position.

Working vertical tucks

Vertical tucks are often used in dressmaking as a method of controlling fullness in a fabric, such as the tucked bodice of a smock or dress where the fabric flows out into a full skirt (see the knitted maternity dress on page 36). Tucks may be knitted into a fabric—usually stockinette stitch—as you work, using a slip stitch technique. Since a knitted fabric is usually quite thick, it is difficult to make a precise-looking vertical tuck similar to a dressmaking one. Instead, depending on the number of stitches used in the tuck and the thickness of the yarn, some larger tucks may look like gently rounded ridges on the surface of the fabric rather than a complete fold.

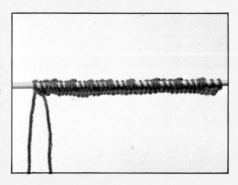

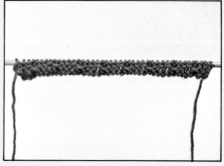

1 In this fabric there are two stitches in each tuck with three stitches between them and at each end. Cast on required number of stitches and work 1st row (RS): K3, *keeping yarn at back, sl next 2 sts purlwise, K3, rep from * to end.

2 After slipping the tuck stitches in RS rows, draw the yarn across as tightly as possible when you knit the following stitches. Work the 2nd row: P to end.

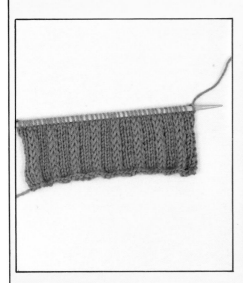

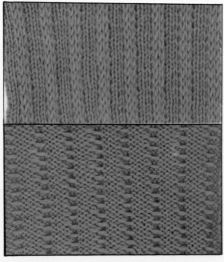

3 Repeat the two pattern rows for the depth of fabric needed. After a few rows have been worked, you can see the slipped stitches forming vertical ridges on the right side of the fabric.

4 When the tucked section is the required depth, bind off after a WS row. Here both sides of the fabric are shown. Note the horizontal strands on the WS where the yarn has been pulled across the slipped stitches.

5 If you are using the tucks as a method of controlling fullness (as on the yoke of a dress) you can continue knitting downward into the skirt in ordinary stockinette stitch. When the tucks are released and the fabric is no longer restrained by the strands of yarn across the slipped stitches, the fabric hangs in gathers or folds if the knitting is in a large piece. The amount of gathering depends on the number of stitches in each tuck and density of tucks on the fabric.

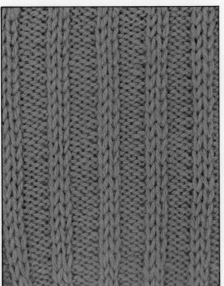

As with horizontal tucks, you can work vertical tucks in varying depths according to the number of stitches used. The tucks become less precise when they are larger, since it is difficult to keep the yarn taut when stretching it across a large number of slipped stitches.

Stockinette stitch tucks are very attractive against a reverse stockinette stitch background. They resemble a ribbed fabric, but are less elastic since the stockinette stitch "ribs" are restrained by the bars of yarn at the back where it passes the slipped stitches.

Working the tucks in a contrasting color is similar to working narrow vertical stripes (see Volume 3, pages 39-41. Start the fabric with an initial WS row, then continue working in the tuck pattern. On RS rows, when slipping stitches, do not use the tuck yarn, but weave it across the back of the fabric. Vertical tucks may be worked in a color different from the background to give a striped effect. In this photograph the "stripes" stand out in light relief.

Mike Berend

Maternity dress and smock

Vertical and horizontal tucks add extra style to this comfortable dress and smock.

Sizes
To fit 32-34[36-38]in (83-87[92-97]cm) bust.
Dress length, 44¼[44½]in (112[113]cm).
Smock length, 30[30½]in (76[77]cm).
Sleeve seam, 6in (15cm).

Materials
24[25]oz (675[700]g) of a sport yarn in main color (A) for dress
21[22]oz (575[600]g) in main color (A) for smock
3oz (75g) each of contrasting colors (B and C) for either garment
1 pair each Nos. 2 and 3 (2¾ and 3¼mm) knitting needles

Gauge
28 stitches and 36 rows to 4in (10cm) in stockinette stitch on No. 3 (3¼mm) knitting needles.

Dress

Back
Using No. 2 (2¾mm) needles and A, cast on 224[233] sts. Beg with a K row, work 15 rows stockinette st.
Next row K to end to mark hemline.
Change to No. 3 (3¼mm) needles. Beg with a K row, work 28 rows stockinette st.
First tuck
Using A, **K1 row, then beg with a K row work 15 rows rev stockinette st.
Next row Fold work to the back and K one st from the needle and one st from the 1st row of tuck to end.**

Chris Harvey

Using A, beg with a P row and work 5 rows stockinette st.
Next row K13[14], *K2 tog, K26[27], rep from * 6 times more, K2 tog, K13[14]. 216[225] sts.
Work 15 more rows stockinette st.
Second tuck
Using B, rep from ** to **, then using A, beg with a P row and work 5 rows stockinette st.
Next row K12[13], *K2 tog, K25[26], rep from * 6 times more, K2 tog, K to end. 208[217] sts.
Work 15 more rows stockinette st.

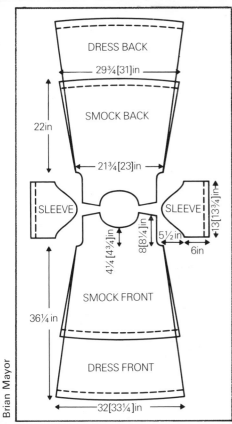

Brian Mayor

Third tuck
Using C, rep from ** to **, then using A, beg with a P row and work 5 rows stockinette st.
Next row K12[13], *K2 tog, K24[25], rep from * 6 times more, K2 tog, K to end. 200[209] sts.
Using A, cont in stockinette st, dec 8 sts evenly across every 40th row until 152[161] sts rem. Cont straight until work measures $36\frac{1}{4}$in (92cm) from hemline; end with a P row.
Shape armholes and beg yoke
1st row Bind off 5, K16[17] (including st on needle), *P5, K10[11], rep from * 6 times more, P5, K to end.
2nd row Bind off 5, P16[17], *sl 5, P10[11], rep from * 6 times more, sl 5, P to end.
3rd row Bind off 2, K14[15], work as 1st row from * to end.
4th row Bind off 2, P14[15], work as 2nd row from * to end.
Keeping patt correct as now set, dec one st at each end of next and foll 4[5] alternate rows. 130[137] sts. Cont straight until armhole measures $4\frac{1}{4}[4\frac{3}{4}]$in (11[12]cm); end with a WS row.
Shape neck
Next row Patt 47[49], turn and leave rem sts on a spare needle.
Complete left side of neck first.
Next row Bind off 2, patt to end.
Next row Patt to last 5 sts, P5 tog. 41[43] sts.
Bind off 2 sts at beg of next and foll 2 alternate rows; end with a RS row. 35[37] sts. Dec one st at beg of next and foll 4[5] alternate rows; end with a WS row. 30[31] sts.
Next row Patt to last 5 sts, P5 tog.
Dec one st at beg of next row, then cont straight until armhole measures $8[8\frac{1}{4}]$in (20[21]cm); end with a WS row.
Shape shoulder
Bind off 5 sts at beg of next and foll alternate row.
Next row P to last 5 sts, K5 tog.
Bind off 5 sts at beg of next row. Work 1 row. Bind off rem 6[7] sts. Return to sts on spare needle. With RS of work facing, rejoin yarn, K8[9], P5 tog, K10[11], P5 tog, K8[9], sl these 28[31] sts onto holder, patt to end.
Next row Patt to end.
Next row Bind off 2, patt to end.
Next row Patt to last 5 sts, K5 tog.
Complete to match first side, reversing all shaping.

Front
Work as for back.

Sleeves
Using No. 2 ($2\frac{3}{4}$mm) needles, A, cast on 92[96] sts. Beg with a K row, work 9 rows stockinette st.
Next row K to end to mark hemline.
Change to No. 3 ($3\frac{1}{4}$mm) needles. Beg with a K row, work 20 rows stockinette st.

Make first tuck in A, then work 15 rows stockinette st in A. Make second tuck in B, then work 15 rows stockinette st in A. Make third tuck in C, then P 1 row in A.
Shape top
Using A throughout, bind off 5 sts at beg of next 2 rows. Dec one st at each end of next and foll 16[18] alternate rows; end with a P row. Bind off 2 sts at beg of next 8 rows, 3 sts at beg of next 4 rows, 4 sts at beg of next 2 rows, then bind off rem 12 sts.

Neckband
Join right shoulder seam. Using No. 2 ($2\frac{3}{4}$mm) needles, A and with RS facing, *pick up and K 44 sts down left front neck, K front neck sts from holder, pick up and K 44 sts up right front neck, rep from * around back neck. 232[238] sts. Beg with a P row, work 8 rows stockinette st. K 1 row to mark hemline. Beg with a K row, work 8 rows stockinette st. Bind off loosely.
To finish
Press or block according to yarn used. Join left shoulder and neckband seam. Fold neckband in half to inside and slip stitch in place. Set in sleeves. Join side and sleeve seams. Turn up hems at lower edge and sleeve edges and slip stitch in place. Press seams.

Smock

Back
Using size 2 ($2\frac{3}{4}$mm) needles and A, cast on 208[217] sts. Beg with a K row work 11 rows stockinette st.
Next row K to end to mark hemline. Change to size 3 ($3\frac{1}{4}$mm) needles. Beg with a K row, work 20 rows stockinette st. Make first tuck as for dress, then using A, work 5 rows stockinette st.
Next row K12[13], *K2 tog, K24[25], rep from * 6 times more, K2 tog, K to end. 200[209] sts. Work 11 more rows stockinette st. Make 2nd tuck as for dress, then using A, work 5 rows stockinette st.
Next row K11[12], *K2 tog, K23[24], rep from * 6 times more, K2 tog, K to end. 192[201] sts. Work 11 more rows stockinette st. Make 3rd tuck as for dress, then using A, work 5 rows stockinette st.
Next row K11[12], *K2 tog, K22[23], rep from * 6 times more, K2 tog, K to end. 184[193] sts.
Using A, cont in stockinette st, dec 8 sts evenly across every 30th row until 152[161] sts rem. Cont straight until work measures 22in (56cm) from hemline; end with a P row. Complete as for dress from *** to end.

Front
Work as for back.

Sleeves, neckband and finishing
Work as for dress.

Knitting/COURSE 52

Introduction to Aran knitting

Some of the most distinctive knitting patterns originated in the coastal villages of Britain and Ireland. The tightly knit "fisherman" sweater provided excellent protection from the elements and, like much traditional peasant craft, became the focus of generations of creative talent. The patterns were never written down but were handed down through families, so that each time one family was joined to another by marriage, the designs were mixed and enhanced. No doubt the Aran Isles, off the west coast of Ireland on the outer edge of Galway Bay, produced the most ornate and complicated patterns. These sweaters were completely covered with a variety of cables and bobbles in high relief, and modern adaptions rarely approach the effect of the densely patterned traditional Aran sweater.

It is said that the Aran fishermen considered it the wife's duty to spin the green, gray, brown or cream wool, while it was the husband's privilege to knit it. So, the stunning and often astoundingly intricate cables of the Aran sweater were devised by men well versed in fishermen's knots and braids. In addition to these cable "ropes", most elements of the designs depicted everyday objects or events. Diamond shapes are thought to suggest the fishing net mesh, bobbles the rocks and berries, seed or moss stitch the local mosses, trellis shapes the fenced fields, honeycomb shapes the bee's nest, zigzags a cliff path, or the ups and downs of marriage.

The following step-by-step instructions show how to work two bobble variations suitable for bobbled fabric (see Volume 6, pages 39-41 or how to work standard bobbles).

38

Crochet-knit bobbles

The standard bobble is either completed over several rows of knitting or completed in one row by turning the work a few times at the bobble. When making a bobbled fabric you may find that it is more convenient to work bobbles that can be completed in one row and without turning, as in the crochet-knit bobble. This bobble gets its name from the fact that it is composed of a chain which, although worked with knitting techniques, is constructed like a crochet chain.

It will not produce a very large or distinctly round bobble but is adequate for a bobbled fabric. Because they add elasticity, panels of allover bobble knitting are often positioned under the arms on the sleeves and bodies of Aran sweaters.

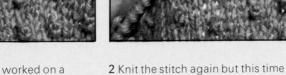

1 This bobble should be worked on a stockinette stitch ground. First knit to the position of the bobble. Then knit the next stitch and slip the stitch just knitted back onto the left-hand needle.

2 Knit the stitch again but this time through the back of the stitch in order to twist it.

3 Repeat this process twice more, slipping the stitch just knitted back onto the left-hand needle and knitting it through the back. This forms the bobble chain.

4 The making of the chain can be speeded up by not actually slipping the stitch each time back onto the left-hand needle. Merely insert left-hand needle into front of stitch just knitted on right-hand needle. Then, without removing left-hand needle, knit left-hand stitch again with right-hand needle.

5 Once the bobble chain is the required length, continue to knit the stockinette stitch ground to the position of the next bobble in the row. In the following row the bobble is purled like the rest of the stitches. There will be a little hole behind the bobble. These holes create the elasticity of bobbled fabric.

6 If the bobbles are worked along every knit row, a bobbled fabric is produced. The texture of the fabric can be made denser by lengthening the crochet-knit chain and more elastic by working the bobbles closer together. See Stitch Wise for Currant stitch and Clove stitch, which use crochet-knit bobbles.

Mike Berend

Terry Evans

Alternative method for making crochet-knit bobbles

1 Another method of working the crochet-knit bobble is by making new stitches with yarn overs instead of knitting into the stitch repeatedly. Knit to the position of the bobble. Knit the next stitch and then bring the yarn forward.

2 Holding the yarn over right-hand needle and at back of work, insert tip of left-hand needle into front of last knit stitch on right-hand needle. Lift stitch over new loop created by the yarn over and off right-hand needle.

3 Repeat this process three more times—making a new loop on the right-hand needle with a yarn over and passing the last stitch over it. The bobble chain looks like the one shown in the basic method but it is slightly looser.

Picot-knot bobbles

This is another example of a bobble which can be completed in the row in which it is begun and without turning the work. The stitches that make up the bobble are added by casting on using the knit cast on method shown in Volume 1, pages 26-27.

1 This bobble is also worked on a stockinette stitch ground. Knit to position of bobble. Then insert right-hand needle into next stitch on left-hand needle and draw a loop through without dropping left-hand stitch on left-hand needle. Return new loop to left-hand needle.

2 Insert the right-hand needle into the new stitch and draw another loop through and return it to the left-hand needle. Cast on two more stitches in this way until there are four new stitches on the left-hand needle.

3 Knit the four new stitches onto the right-hand needle in the usual way. The fifth stitch, the original stitch, should be dropped from the left-hand needle.

4 Using the tip of the left-hand needle, lift the second stitch on the right-hand needle over the first and off the right-hand needle. Then lift the third stitch over the first, and lastly the fourth over the first. This completes the picot-knot bobble.

5 The sample above shows picot-knot bobbles on every fourth stitch in a row with each row of bobbles separated by 3 plain rows of stockinette stitch. By working the bobbles closer together in the row and by separating the bobble rows with only one plain row, you can produce a denser fabric.

Mike Berend

Stitch Wise

Marriage lines

Cast on a panel of 14 sts.
1st row (RS) K2, P1, K1, P1, K9.
2nd row P8, K1, P1, K1, P3.
3rd row K4, P1, K1, P1, K7.
4th row P6, K1, P1, K1, P5.
5th row K6, P1, K1, P1, K5.
6th row P4, K1, P1, K1, P7.
7th row K8, P1, K1, P1, K3.
8th row P2, K1, P1, K1, P9.
9th, 10th, 11th, 12th, 13th and 14th rows
Work as 7th, 6th, 5th, 4th, 3rd and 2nd rows.
These 14 rows form patt.

Currant stitch

Cast on a multiple of 4 sts plus 3 extra.
1st row (WS) P to end.
2nd row K3, * K next st, (sl st just knitted back to left-hand needle and K it again through back) 3 times, K3, rep from * to end.
3rd row P to end.
4th row K1, *K next st 4 times as in 2nd row, K3, rep from * ending last repeat K1.
These 4 rows form patt.

Clove stitch

Cast on an odd number of sts.
1st row (WS) P to end.
2nd row *K2, (yo to make new st, pass last st over new st) 4 times, rep from * to last st, K1.
3rd row P to end.
4th row K1, rep from * of 2nd row to last 2 sts, K2.
These 4 rows form patt.

Speck stitch

Cast on a multiple of 6 sts plus 1 extra.
1st row and all odd numbered rows (WS) P to end.
2nd row K to end.
4th row K3, *insert right-hand needle under running thread between 1st and 2nd sts on left-hand needle, draw through a loop, insert right-hand needle between same sts above running thread, draw through another loop, P first st on left-hand needle, yarn to back, with left-hand needle lift first loop over 2nd loop and pulled st and off needle, pass 2nd loop over purled st and off needle, K5, rep from *, end last rep K3.
6th row K to end.
8th row K6, rep from * of 4th row to last st, K1. These 8 rows form patt.

Seed stitch diamonds

Cast on a panel of 17 sts.
1st row (RS) K8, P1, K8.
2nd row P7, K1, P1, K1, P7.
3rd row K6, P1, (K1, P1) twice, K6.
4th row P5, (K1, P1) 3 times, K1, P5.
5th row K4, P1, (K1, P1) 4 times, K4.
6th row P3, (K1, P1) 5 times, K1, P3.
7th row K2, P1, (K1, P1) 6 times, K2.
8th row (P1, K1) 8 times, P1.
9th, 10th, 11th, 12th, 13th and 14th rows
Work as 7th, 6th, 5th, 4th, 3rd and 2nd rows.
These 14 rows form patt.

Framed bobble

Cast on a multiple of 6 sts plus 1 extra.
1st, 2nd and 3rd rows P to end.
4th row (RS) P1, *K5, P1, rep from * to end.
5th row P to end.
6th row P1, *K2, K into front, back, front of next st, turn and P3. Using point of left-hand needle, lift 2nd and 3rd sts separately over first and off right-hand needle—called make bobble (MB)—K2, P1, rep from * to end.
7th row P to end.
8th row Rep 4th row.
These 8 rows form patt.

Simon Butcher

Bobble jackets

Be a sport. Make one of these bobble jackets to keep you warm on the golf course.

Sizes
To fit 32-34[36-38:40-42]in (83-87[92-97:102-107]cm) bust/chest.
Length, 24[25½:26½]in (61[64:67]cm).
Sleeve seam, 17¼[18:18½]in (44[46:47]cm).
Note Directions for larger sizes are in brackets []; if there is only one set of figures it applies to all sizes.

Materials
32[36:38]oz (900[1000:1050]g) of a knitting worsted
1 pair each Nos. 6 and 8 (4½ and 5½mm) knitting needles
Cable needle
6 buttons

Gauge
16 sts and 30 rows to 4in (10cm) in rev stockinette st on No. 8 (5½mm) needles.

Back
Using No. 6 (4½mm) needles cast on 70[82:90] sts.
1st row K2, *P2, K2, rep from * to end.
2nd row P2, *K2, P2, rep from * to end.
Rep these 2 rows for 4in (10cm); end with a 2nd row and inc 3[1:3] sts evenly across last row. 73[83:93] sts. Change to No. 8 (5½mm) needles. P1 row and K1 row. Beg patt.
1st row (RS) P9[11:13], (K1, P1, K1, P1, K1) all into next st, turn and beg with a P row work 6 rows rev stockinette st, then sl 2nd, 3rd, 4th and 5th sts over first st on needle—called make bobble (MB)—, *P17[19:21], MB, rep from * twice, P9 [11:13].
2nd row K8[10:12], P1, K1, P1, *K15 [17:19], P1, K1, P1, rep from * twice, K8[10:12].

3rd row P7[9:11], sl next st onto cable needle and leave at back of work, K1, then P st from cable needle—called cross right (CR)—P1, sl next st onto cable needle and leave at front of work, P1, then K st from cable needle—called cross left (CL)—*P13[15:17], CR, P1, CL, rep from * twice, P7[9:11].

4th row K7[9:11], P1, K3, P1, *K13 [15:17], P1, K3, P1, rep from * twice, K7[9:11].

5th row P6[8:10], CR, P3, CL, *P11 [13:15], CR, P3, CL, rep from * twice, P6[8:10].

6th row K6[8:10], P1, K5, P1, *K11 [13:15], P1, K5, P1, rep from * twice, K6[8:10].

7th row P5[7:9], CR, P5, CL, *P9 [11:13], CR, P5, CL, rep from * twice, P5[7:9].

8th row K5[7:9], P1, K7, P1, *K9 [11:13], P1, K7, P1, rep from * twice, K5[6:7].

9th row P4[6:8], CR, P7, CL, *P7[9:11], CR, P7, CL, rep from * twice, P4[6:8].

10th row K4[6:8], P1, K9, P1, *K7[9:11], P1, K9, P1, rep from * twice, K4[6:8].

11th row P3[5:7], CR, P9, CL, *P5[7:9], CR, P9, CL, rep from * twice, P3[5:7].

12th row K3[5:7], P1, K11, P1, *K5 [7:9], P1, K11, P1, rep from * twice, K3[5:7].

13th row P2[4:6], CR, P11, CL, *P3 [5:7], CR, P11, CL, rep from * twice, P2[4:6].

14th row K2[4:6], P1, K13, P1, *K3[5:7], P1, K13, P1, rep from * twice, K2[4:6].

15th row P2[4:6], MB, P13, MB, *P3 [5:7], MB, P13, MB, rep from * twice, P2[4:6].

16th-29th rows Work from 14th row back to 1st row, reading CL for CR and CR for CL.

30th-36th rows Beg with a K row, work 7 rows rev stockinette st.

37th row P18[21:24], *MB, P17[19:21], rep from * twice, P1[2:3]. This row sets the patt for the next block of diamonds.

38th-72nd rows Work diamond patt and 7 rows rev stockinette as set.

These 72 rows form the patt and are rep throughout the back. Cont in patt until work measures 24[25¼:26½]in (61[64: 67]cm); end with a WS row.

Shape shoulders

Bind off 5[6:7] sts at beg of next 8 rows and 5 sts at beg of foll 2 rows. Bind off rem 23[25:27] sts.

Left front

Using No. 8 (5½mm) needles cast on 23[26:29] sts for pocket lining. Beg with a P row, work 29 rows rev stockinette st; end with a P row. Cut off yarn and leave sts on a holder.

Using No. 6 (4½mm) needles cast on 34[38:46] sts. Rib 4in (10cm) for back, inc 3[4:1] sts evenly across last row. 37[42:47] sts. Change to No. 8 (5½mm) needles. P 1 row and K 1 row. Beg patt.

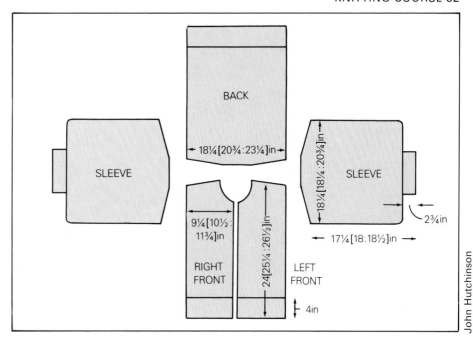

BACK

18¼[20¾:23¼]in

SLEEVE

SLEEVE

18¼[18¼:20¾]in

9¼[10½: 11¾]in

24[25¼:26½]in

RIGHT FRONT

LEFT FRONT

2¾in

17¼[18:18½]in

4in

John Hutchinson

1st row (RS) P9[11:13], MB, P17 [19:21], MB, P9[10:11].

The last row sets the patt for the first block of diamonds. Patt a further 28 rows.

Pocket row K7[8:9], sl next 23[26:29] sts onto a holder, K across sts of pocket lining, K to end of row.

Cont in patt, setting patt for next block of diamonds on 37th row as foll: P18 [21:24], MB, P18[20:22]. Cont in patt until 12[13:14] rows less than back to shoulder shaping have been worked.

Shape neck

Dec one st at neck edge on next 12[13:14] rows.

Shape shoulder

Bind off 5[6:7] sts at beg of next and 3 foll alternate rows. Work 1 row. Bind off rem 5 sts.

Right front

Work as for left front, reversing all shapings.

Sleeves

Using No. 6 (4½mm) needles cast on 50[50:58] sts. Rib 2¾in (7cm) as for back; end with a first row.

Inc row Rib 3[3:4], *pick up loop lying between needles and K tbl—called make 1 (M1)—rib 2, rep from * to last 3[3:4] sts, M1, rib 3[3:4]. 73[73:83] sts. Change to No. 8 (5½mm) needles. Cont as for 1st [1st:2nd] size of back until sleeve measures 17¼[18:18½]in (44[46:47]cm); end with a WS row.

Shape top

Bind off 5 sts at beg of next 12 rows. Bind off rem 13[13:23] sts.

Collar

Using No. 6 (4½mm) needles cast on 106[110:114] sts. Rib 4in (10cm) as for back; end with a 2nd row.

Bind off 10 sts at beg of next 10 rows.

Bind off rem 6[10:14] sts.

Pocket tops

Using No. 6 (4½mm) needles K across sts on holder, inc 3[4:5] sts across row. 26[30:34] sts. Beg with a 2nd row, rib 6 rows as for back. Bind off in ribbing.

Woman's right front band

Using No. 6 (4½mm) needles and with RS facing, pick up and K 98[102:106] sts up right front to beg of neck. Beg with a 2nd row, rib 7 rows as for back.

1st buttonhole row Rib 7[6:8], *bind off 4, rib a further 11[12:12] sts, rep from * to last 11[11:13] sts, bind off 4, rib to end.

2nd buttonhole row Rib to end, casting on 4 sts over those bound off in previous row.

Rib 7 more rows.

Bind off in ribbing.

Woman's left front band

Work as right band, except omitting buttonholes.

Man's left front band

Work as given for woman's right front band, picking up sts along left front and working 1st buttonhole row as foll: rib 7[7:9], *bind off 4, rib a further 11[12:12] sts, rep from * to last 11 [10:12] sts, bind off 4, rib to end.

Man's right front band

Work as left band, except omitting buttonholes.

To finish

Block work. Sew pocket linings and tops in place. Join shoulders. Set in sleeves. Join side sleeve seams. Beg and finish at center of front bands, ease bound-off edge of collar onto neck and sew in place. Sew on buttons.

Shoestring

Cozy cat

Our sleeping cat neatly holds a hot water bottle.

Finished size
$16\frac{1}{2} \times 9\frac{1}{2}$in (42.5 × 24cm).
A seam allowance of $\frac{3}{8}$in (1cm) is included.

Materials
*Piece of red and white gingham
  22 × 20in (55 × 50cm)
Piece of iron-on interfacing 22 × 20in
  (55 × 50cm)
Black and white embroidery floss
$\frac{3}{4}$yd (.6m) of white cord
Matching sewing thread*

1 From gingham cut one piece 20 × 17½in (50 × 45cm) for body.
2 From interfacing cut one piece the same size as the gingham body.
3 From remaining gingham cut out four equilateral triangles, with all sides measuring 3in (8cm), for ears.
4 From interfacing cut out two ears the same size as the gingham ears.
5 Place interfacing ears, shiny side down, on wrong sides of two gingham ears, matching all edges. Iron in place.
6 Using six strands of black embroidery floss, work a line of stem stitch on two adjoining edges of one interfaced ear,

$\frac{3}{4}$in (2cm) in from the edges.
7 Place an interfaced ear on one remaining ear, right sides together and edges matching. Pin, baste and stitch along the two embroidered edges only. Trim seam and turn the ear right side out.
8 Run a line of gathering stitches along the combined raw edges. Pull up the gathering slightly and fasten off.
9 Repeat steps 6 to 8 to make the other ear in the same way.
10 Place interfacing body, shiny side down, on wrong side of fabric body, matching all the edges. Iron in place.
11 Fold body in half lengthwise to form one piece 10 × 17½in (25 × 45cm). With folded edge at the top, round off two corners on one short side for the head end.
12 Position the two ears between the folded fabric on each side of the open rounded corner, with the points inward and the embroidered side of ears facing the right way (see photo).
13 Pin, baste and stitch the rounded side and lower edges, leaving short straight edge open. Overcast the raw edges together to finish. Turn cat right side out.
14 At the open end, form a casing by

turning under the raw edge for $\frac{1}{4}$in (5mm) and then for $\frac{3}{8}$in (1cm). Pin, baste and stitch around casing close to fold, leaving a 1in (2.5cm) opening in the stitching at lower edge.
15 Thread cord through the casing from opening to opening. Knot cord ends together. Fray cord to form a tassel.
16 Using a soft pencil, draw a neat arc for the cat's face, extending it from ear to ear and about 5in (12cm) down from the top edge.
17 Inside the curve, using the soft pencil, draw a $\frac{3}{8}$in (1cm)-diameter circle for a nose, two semicircles for eyes and a semicircle for a mouth. Draw 1½in (4cm)-long whiskers on each side of the nose.
18 On the lower edge, draw four 1½in (4cm)-high arcs for legs in two sets at each end, leaving a gap of about 2½in (6cm) in between each set.
19 Using six strands of black embroidery floss, work eyes, nose, mouth, face and legs in stem stitch.
20 Using six strands of white embroidery floss, work whiskers in stem stitch. Keep one hand inside the bag as you work, so that the embroidery goes through only one layer of fabric.

Spike Powell

* Aran cables
* Adding cable panels to plain knitting
* Working cable panels side by side
* Detached plaits
* Stitch Wise: more cable patterns
* Patterns for a cabled sweater, hat and leg warmers

Aran cables

Despite the variety and complexity of Aran cables, they are all based on the simple principle of slipping stitches onto a cable needle and thereby crossing them over or under other stitches.

Cable variations can be grouped into seven categories. First there are the *single stitch cables* which are made by crossing one stitch over another (see Volume 5, page 52. *Simple cables*, the most common cables, have two knit ribs of two or more stitches each twisted across each other (see Volume 6, pages 34-35). Knit ribs, which wave back and forth without being twisted in the usual way around others, produce *wave cables*. In *double cables* three ribs form repeated horseshoe shapes, and in *chain cables* ribs form chain-link shapes. *Plait cables* are made by using three or more knit ribs and crossing them at intervals like rope plaits. Last and most intricate are the *braid cables*. These beautiful cables are composed of knit ribs which travel across a reverse stockinette stitch background and twist and cross each other intermittently with superb effect.

Generally, Aran cables are worked in panels on a reverse stockinette stitch background, with the width of the panel depending on the type of cable. The step-by-step instructions in this course illustrate how cable panels can be inserted into plain knitting and how a more advanced knitter can create a sweater covered with cables in the fashion of the traditional fisherman's Aran.

Keep in mind that, although cables can be loosely knitted on large needles to produce a slightly open fabric, a tighter cable enhances the sculptural quality of the work.

Adding cable panels to plain knitting

A cable panel can give an interesting highlight to stockinette stitch knitting and can be added to a simple pattern with little difficulty, as shown here. Remember that a single cable panel need not just be used down the side of a cardigan. It can be added down the center of a sleeve or a pocket, worked horizontally across a yoke or around hat bands, socks or gloves; or repeated in between the knit ribs of ribbing at the wrist, hips and neck. The only thing that has to be taken into account is that, although the number of rows to the inch or centimeter for a cable pattern will be nearly the same as that for the stockinette stitch, the cables do tend to pull the width of the fabric together. Therefore more stitches per inch or centimeter will be needed for the panel, and you should check your stitch gauge carefully before beginning pattern.

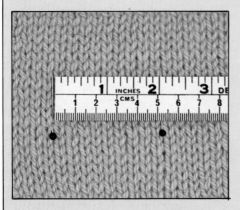

1 First make a sample swatch of plain stockinette stitch using the correct yarn and needles for the pattern you are using. Check your gauge and correct it if necessary by altering the needle size. (See Volume 2, page 27 for a more detailed account of checking gauge.)

2 Next choose your cable panel and make a sample swatch of it using the yarn and needles you are using for the stockinette stitch. Cast on enough stitches to make several plain knitted stitches on each side of the cable panel and work a swatch at least 2in (5cm) deep, or one cable pattern repeat.

3 When the cable sample is completed, bind off the stitches and press the stockinette stitch lightly on the wrong side under a damp cloth. Make sure the swatch is blocked out and flat, but be careful not to stretch it.

continued

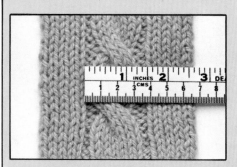

4 Next lay sample RS up on a flat surface and measure width of cable panel. Then calculate how many stitches you will have to add to compensate for panel. If, for example, your gauge for the stockinette stitch is 16 sts to 2in (5cm) and your panel measures 2in (5cm) but takes 20 sts, you will need to add 4 extra stitches for the cable. If your panel measures 1in (2.5cm) and takes 10 sts, add 2 extra stitches for cable panel.

5 It is best to add the extra stitches for the cable panel after the ribbing so as not to alter the width of the ribbing. For instance, when adding a cable panel up the center of a sleeve, work the ribbing at the cuff following your pattern. Then in the first row of the stockinette stitch add the extra stitches for the cable panel at the base of the cable panel.

6 Do not forget to add enough extra stitches to compensate for each cable panel. If the cable panel you are using takes two more stitches per panel and you are working two panels on the front of a pullover, add two extra stitches at the base of each panel after the ribbing is completed.

Working cable panels side by side

You may want to cover your knitting with cables in the manner of the traditional Aran sweater. This needs a bit of extra planning but is not as difficult as it looks. The principle is the same as for adding single panels. These step-by-step instructions show how to plan and arrange a series of cable panels. The one difficulty to bear in mind when working several different cable panels side by side is that the number of rows to complete a pattern repeat may vary. You will therefore have to keep a record while knitting of which row you are working in each pattern.

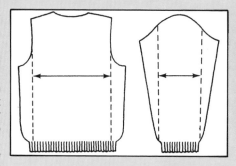

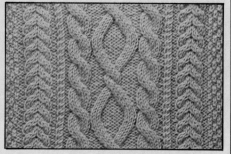

1 It is easiest to run the cable panels across the sweater back and front, stopping at the edge of the armhole so that you do not have to worry about the cable confusing you when you are decreasing for the armhole. On the sleeve the panels can be placed across the width at the wrist. You can easily cover the whole of a T-shape sweater with cables.

2 Once you have calculated the width that your cable panels will cover, you can begin choosing cable patterns. A wide panel is best for the center of the sleeves and bodice. Place narrower panels on each side of the central one, working outward. Vary the texture and type of cable so that each panel offers a sharp contrast to its neighbor.

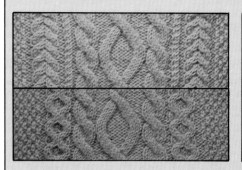

3 Next make sample swatches of the cables you want to use and measure their widths. If you find that the panels worked side by side will be too wide for your purposes you will have to substitute panels of a different design.

4 If the combined panels are too narrow to cover the width, you could add a narrow panel of single bobbles between two panels on each side, or you could separate the cables with a wider reverse stockinette stitch panel.

5 The areas not to be covered with cables should be worked in a complementary texture such as a bobbled fabric, a seed stitch or another simple knit and purl variation. You will have to make a separate stitch swatch for this and adapt it to your pattern.

Detached plaits

This highly embossed cable is made with three knit ribs which cross over and twist around each other alternately. It is worked slightly differently from an ordinary cable; the ribs are worked over more rows than the background and the crossings of the ribs are completed in two rows instead of one. The cables are worked on a reverse stockinette stitch background.

1 The cable is worked over 12 knit stitches on a reverse stockinette stitch background. To try a sample of the cable first work a few rows of reverse stockinette stitch with a central panel of 12 stitches stockinette stitch. Then on the right side, purl across the border and knit the first 8 sts of the stockinette stitch panel. Then (turn, P4, turn, K4) 3 times and slip these 4 sts onto a cable needle and leave at front of work.

2 Pass the yarn to the back of the work between the needles and slip 4 sts from right-hand needle to left-hand needle. Knit across the 8 sts on left-hand needle, then complete the row by purling across the border stitches.

3 On the next row (WS) knit across the border, purl the 8 sts of the cable panel and purl the 4 sts from the cable needle. Then complete the row by knitting the rest of the border stitches.

4 On the 3rd row purl the border stitches. Knit over the first 8 sts of the cable panel, then (turn, P4, turn, K4) 3 times and slip these 4 sts onto the cable needle and leave at front of work. Pass the yarn to the back of the work and slip 4 sts from left-hand needle to right-hand needle. Purl border stitches to complete row.

5 On the following row (WS) knit the border stitches. Purl the 4 sts from cable needle. Then purl the next 8 sts of the cable panel and complete the row by knitting the border stitches.
These four rows form the pattern.

6 The thick cable stands out in high relief from the reverse stockinette stitch background. If you are working several of these cables side by side, you will need several short cable needles, since the stitches slipped onto the cable needle are not knitted off until the return row.

Mike Berend

Stitch Wise

Deer cable

Cast on a panel of 20 sts.
1st row (WS) K2, P16, K2.
2nd row P2, K4, sl next 2 sts onto cable needle (cn) and leave at back of work, K2, then K2 from cn—called cable 4 back or C4B—, sl next 2 sts onto cn and leave at front of work, K2, then K2 from cn—called cable 4 front or C4F—, K4, P2.
3rd row As 1st.
4th row P2, K2, C4B, K4, C4F, K2, P2.
5th row As 1st.
6th row P2, C4B, K8, C4F, P2.
These 6 rows form patt.

Ribbed cable

Cast on a panel of 11 sts.
1st row (WS) K2, (P1 tbl, K1) 3 times, P1 tbl, K2.
2nd row P2, sl next 3 sts onto cable needle (cn) and leave at front of work, (K1 tbl, P1) twice, K1 tbl, P1, K1 tbl from cn, P2.
3rd, 5th, 7th and 9th rows As 1st.
4th, 6th, 8th and 10th rows P2, (K1 tbl, P1) 3 times, K1 tbl, P2.
These 10 rows form patt.

Rope braid

Cast on a panel of 16 sts.
1st row (WS) K5, P6, K5.
2nd row P5, K2, sl next 2 sts onto cable needle (cn) and leave at back of work, K2, then K2 from cn, P5.
3rd and every alternate row K all knit sts and P all purl sts.
4th row P5, sl next 2 sts onto cn and leave at front of work, K2, then K2 from cn, K2, P5.
6th row As 2nd.
8th row As 4th.
10th row As 2nd.
12th row As 4th.
14th row P4, sl next st onto cn and leave at back of work, K2, then P1 from cn—called back cross or BC—, K2, sl next 2 sts onto cn and leave at front of work, P1, then K2 from cn—called front cross or FC—, P4.
16th row P3, BC, P1, K2, P1, FC, P3.
18th row P2, BC, P2, K2, P2, FC, P2.
20th row P2, FC, P2, K2, P2, BC, P2.
22nd row P3, FC, P1, K2, P1, BC, P3.
24th row P4, FC, K2, BC, P4.
These 24 rows form patt.

Cabled sweater, hat and leg warmers

Knit a set of winter warmers to keep out the cold.

Sizes
Sweater To fit 26[28:30:32:34:36:38]in (66[71:76:83:87:92:97]cm) chest/bust.
Length, 18[18¾:20½:21½:23½:24½:25¾]in (45.5[47.5:52:54:59.5:61.5:65]cm).
Sleeve, 13[14:15:16:16½:17:17]in (33[36:39:41:42:43:43]cm).
Hat To fit average size head.
Leg warmers Small [medium:large].
Note: Directions for larger sizes are in brackets []; if there is only one set of figures it applies to all sizes.

Materials
20[22:24:27:30:32:34] oz (580[630: 690:780:860:920:980]g) of a bulky pure wool yarn
1 pair each Nos. 10 and 11 (6½ and 7½mm) knitting needles
Set of four No. 11 (7½mm) needles
1 cable needle (cn)

Gauge
12 sts and 16 rows to 4in (10cm) in stockinette st on No. 11 (7½mm) needles.

Sweater

Back and front (alike)
Lower section
Using No. 10 (6½mm) needles cast on 44[48:50:54:56:60:62] sts.
Work 6[6:8:8:10:10:10] rows K1, P1 ribbing but for 1st, 3rd, 5th and 7th sizes only inc one st at end of last row.
45[48:51:54:57:60:63] sts.
Change to No. 11 (7½mm) needles. Beg with a K row, work 4[4:6:6:8:8:10] rows stockinette st. Bind off.
Cable band
Using No. 11 (7½mm) needles cast on 12 sts.
1st row K to end.
2nd row K1, P10, K1.
3rd row K3, *place next 2 sts on cn and leave at front of work, K2, then K the sts from cn—called cable 4 front or C4F—, rep from * once more, K1.
4th row K1, P10, K1.
5th row K1, *place next 2 sts on cn and leave at back of work, K2, then K the sts from cn—called cable 4 back or C4B—, rep from * once more, K3.
6th row K1, P10, K1.
Rows 3 to 6 from patt. Cont in patt until band measures 14[15:16:17:18:19:20]in (36[38:41:43:46:48:51]cm). Bind off.
Join bound-off edge of lower section to one long edge of cable band. With RS facing and using No. 11 (7½mm) needle pick up and K 45[48:51:54:57:60:63] sts

evenly along other edge of band. Beg
with a P row, work 15[17:19:21:23:25:
27] rows stockinette st. Bind off.
Work another cable band and sew to
bound-off edge of stockinette st section.
Sleeves and yoke
Using No. 11 (7½mm) needles cast on
34[36:38:40:42:44:46] sts.
1st row (RS) P11[12:13:14:15:16:17],
K12, P11[12:13:14:15:16:17].

2nd row K11[12:13:14:15:16:17], P12,
K11[12:13:14:15:16:17].
3rd and 4th rows As 1st and 2nd.
5th row P11[12:13:14:15:16:17],
place next 3 sts on cn and leave at
back of work, K3, then K the sts from cn—
called cable 6 back or C6B—, place next
3 sts on cn and leave at front of work,
K3, then K the sts from cn—called cable
6 front or C6F—, P11[12:13:14:15:16:
17].

17].
6th row As 2nd.
7th-12th rows As 1st-6th.
13th-16th rows 1st and 2nd rows twice.
17th row P11[12:13:14:15:16:17],
C6F, C6B, P11[12:13:14:15:16:17].
19th-24th rows As 13th-18th.
These 24 rows form patt. Cont in patt,
inc one st at each end of next and every
foll 6th[6th:6th:6th:8th:8th:8th] row

Kim Sayer

49

until there are 42[44:46:48:52:54:56] sts. Mark each end of last row to denote position of first dec row of left sleeve. Cont straight for 72[78:84:90:92:96:96] rows.

Divide for neck opening
Work 17[18:18:19:20:21:22], bind off 8[8:10:10:12:12:12], work to end.
Work on first set of 17[18:18:19:20: 21:22] sts thus:
Next row K to last 2 sts, K2 tog.
Next row P to end.
Rep last 2 rows once. Cont in reverse stockinette st on rem 15[16:16:17: 18:19:20] sts, work 14[14:16:16:18: 18:20] rows.
Inc row K to last st, inc in last st.
Next row P to end.
Rep inc row once more. Cut off yarn. Rejoin yarn to front neck edge.
Next row K to end.
Next row P to last 2 sts, P2 tog.
Rep last 2 rows until 12[13:13:14:15: 16:17] sts rem. Work 4[4:6:6:8:8:10] rows stockinette st.
Inc row Inc in first st, K to end.
Next row P to end.
Rep last 2 rows 3 times, then the inc row again. 17[18:18:19:20:21:22] sts, turn and cast on 8[8:10:10:12:12:12], then work across sts of other side of yoke. 42[44:46:48:52:54:56] sts.
Cont in cable patt as right sleeve, dec one st at each end of row that corresponds with marked row on right sleeve and then on every foll 6th[6th:6th:6th:8th:8th: 8th] row until 34[36:38:40:42:44:46] sts rem. Patt 24 rows. Bind off.

To finish
Press with warm iron over a damp cloth. Sew yoke to top edge of back and front, then join side and sleeve seams.

Cuffs (alike)
Using No. 11 (7½mm) needles cast on 12[12:12:16:16:16:16] sts.
1st row K.
2nd row K2, P to last 2 sts, K2.
3rd and 4th rows As 1st and 2nd.
5th row K2, C4B[C4B:C4B:C6B:C6B: C6B:C6B], C4F[C4F:C4F:C6F:C6F: C6F:C6F], K2.
6th row K2, P to last 2 sts, K2.
7th and 8th rows As 1st and 2nd.
Rep 1st-6th rows for 1st, 2nd and 3rd sizes and 1st-8th rows for 4th, 5th, 6th and 7th sizes until cuff fits around sleeve edge; end with a 6th[6th:6th:8th:8th: 8th:8th] patt row. Bind off. Join cast-on and bound-off edges of cuffs tog. Sew on cuffs, then turn back.

Collar
Using 3 of No. 11 (7½mm) set of needles pick up and K 56[56:60:60:68:72:76] sts evenly around neck edge. Work in K1, P1 ribbing for 6[6:7:7:8:8:9]in (15[15:18:18:20:20:23]cm). Bind off in ribbing.

Hat

Using No. 11 (7½mm) needles cast on 12[12:12:16:16:16:16] sts. Work in cable patt as for cuffs until 11 patts have been worked. Bind off but do not cut off yarn, pick up and K 54[54:54:60:60:60: 60] sts along edge of band. Beg with knit row, work in stockinette st for 20[20:20:24:24:24:24] rows.
Shape crown
1st row (K4, K2 tog) to end.
2nd and every other row P to end.
3rd row (K3, K2 tog) to end.
5th row (K2, K2 tog) to end.
7th row (K1, K2 tog) to end.
9th row (K2 tog) to end.

Thread yarn end through rem sts, gather up tightly and secure. Join back seam. Fold back brim. Make pompom and attach.

Leg warmers

Using No. 11 (7½mm) needles cast on 12[12:16] sts. Work cable band as for cuff until 7[8:7] patts have been worked. Bind off but do not cut off yarn, pick up and K 34[38:42] sts along edge of band. Work 18[22:26] rows K1, P1 ribbing. Cont to rib dec one st at each end of next and every foll 4th row until 24[28:30] sts rem. Work 2[2:4] rows. Bind off in ribbing. Join seams.

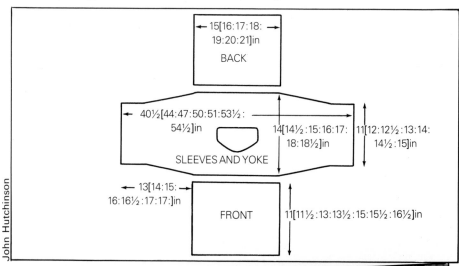

John Hutchinson

Kim Sayer

Knitting / COURSE 54

Allover Aran cable stitches

Aran knitting is noted not only for its vast range of cable panels but also for many allover cable stitch patterns. Some of these cabled fabrics closely resemble cable panels, in that the ribs travel across the background, crossing or twisting at intervals. Others, although created using the same technique of crossing stitches, bear very little resemblance to cable panels except that they, too, are highly embossed. A good example of this is Aran honeycomb and its variations. Allover cable patterns (see Stitch Wise) are actually very helpful to the knitter who needs a cable panel of a specific width. Whereas patterns for standard cable panels can be widened only by repeating the whole panel, allover cable patterns can be used to create panels of varying widths merely by adding one or more widthwise repeats. The step-by-step directions that follow explain how to make single stitch ribs travel across the background knitting and how to work Aran honeycomb.

Traveling single stitch ribs

Single stitch ribs are the basis of a variety of patterns. In Volume 5, pages 52-53 the methods for twisting stitches to form tiny cables are given. The most effective designs created by twisted stitches, however, are those which are formed by traveling lines. These step-by-step directions show how a single stitch rib can be made to travel across the background knitting. Simple cables with larger ribs travel using the same principle, but a cable needle must be used.

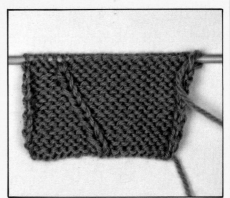

Mike Berend

1 Work a few rows of reverse stockinette stitch with a single knit stitch rib going up the center. Then on the right side purl to the knit stitch, skip the knit stitch and purl into the back of the second stitch leaving it on the left-hand needle.

2 Knit the stitch that was skipped and slip both stitches from the left-hand needle together. This produces the **left cross**.

3 To make the rib travel across the background to the left, work left twists as in steps 1 and 2 on every right-side row. On the wrong-side rows knit all the knit stitches and purl the single stitch rib.

continued

4 For a right twist, purl the background on a right-side row to one stitch before the knit stitch rib. Skip the next stitch (a purl stitch) and knit the second stitch (the knit stitch rib) leaving it on the needle.

5 Purl the stitch that was skipped and slip both stitches from the needle together. This produces the **right cross.**

6 To make the rib travel across the background to the right, work right twists as in steps 4 and 5 on every right-side row. On the wrong-side rows knit all the knit stitches and purl the single stitch rib.

Alternative method for traveling single stitch ribs

Traveling single stitch rib cables, unlike wider cables, aren't necessarily worked on a reverse stockinette stitch background. The standard method for crossing traveling single stitch ribs on a plain stockinette stitch background is the same as that shown in Volume 5, pages 52-53 for ordinary single stitch rib cables.

As the alternative method shown here may be faster for some knitters, it could be more convenient for working allover twisted stitch patterns. The best thing to do is to try this method and the standard method and then decide which one you prefer.

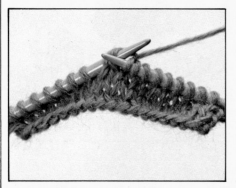

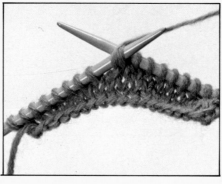

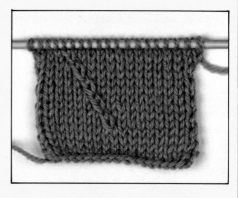

1 For a **left cross** knit background stitches up to single stitch rib. Skip next stitch (the rib stitch). Then with right-hand needle behind left-hand needle knit 2nd stitch through back loop.

2 Then knit both stitches (the stitch that was skipped and the second stitch) together through the back. This completes the left cross.

3 To make the single rib travel to the left across the background, work left crosses on every right-side row and purl all wrong-side rows.

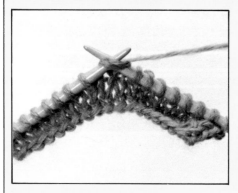

4 For a **right cross,** knit the background stitches up to one stitch before the single stitch rib. Knit the next two stitches together and leave them on left-hand needle.

5 Insert right-hand needle from front between two stitches just knitted together and knit first stitch again. Then slip both stitches from left-hand needle together. This completes right cross.

6 To make the single rib travel to the right across the background, work right crosses on every right-side row and purl all wrong-side rows.

Aran honeycomb

Aran honeycomb is one of the best-known allover cable stitch patterns. At first glance the embossed surface of this stitch is not easily related to that of simple cables. But it is in fact composed of chain cables worked side by side with no inter-vening background stitches to separate them.

Chain cables in turn consist of two wave cables which are two ribs that do not twist but merely wave back and forth one under the other. This is a good example of both the simplicity and the scope of a basic cable technique.

The step-by-step directions given here show how to work a chain cable and therefore the Aran honeycomb variations which derive from it.

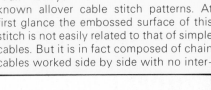

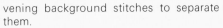

1 To make a sample of a chain cable panel, first work a few rows of an eight-stitch panel bordered by reverse stockinette stitch on each side. Then on a right-side row purl across the border. Slip the next two stitches onto the cable needle and leave them at back of work. Knit the next two stitches, then knit the two stitches from the cable needle.

2 Slip the next two stitches onto the cable needle and leave them at the front of the work. Knit the next two stitches, then knit the two stitches from the cable needle. To complete the row purl across the border.

3 The chain cable is crossed on every 4th row. Work the next three rows without crossing. Purl all purl stitches and knit all knit stitches.

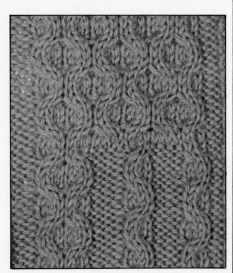

4 On the fourth row (right side) purl the border stitches. Slip the next two stitches onto the cable needle and leave at front of work. Knit the next two stitches. Knit the two stitches from the cable needle.

5 Slip the next two stitches onto the cable needle and leave at back of work. Knit the next two stitches, then knit the two stitches from the cable needle. This forms the characteristic circular center of the chain cable.

Work the next three rows, again without crossing, before knitting from step 1 as before.

6 The sample above illustrates how two simple wave cables (bottom right) worked side by side form the chain cable (bottom left). When chain cables are worked repeatedly side by side with no intervening background, Aran honeycomb is produced (top).

Mike Berend

Stitch Wise

T2L—K 2nd st on left-hand needle through back of loop, K first st, sl both sts from left-hand needle.
T2R—K 2nd st on left-hand needle, K first st, sl both sts from left-hand needle.

Net lattice

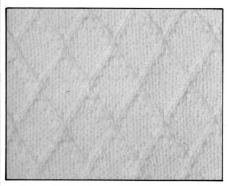

Cast on a multiple of 16 sts plus 2 extra.
1st and every foll alternate row P to end.
2nd row K1, *T2L, K4, T2R, rep from * to last st, K1.
4th row K2, *T2L, K2, T2R, K2, rep from * to end.
6th row K3, *T2L, T2R, K4, rep from * ending last repeat K3.
8th row K4, *T2R, K6, rep from * ending last repeat K4.
10th row K3, *T2R, T2L, K4, rep from * ending last repeat K3.
12th row K2, *T2R, K2, T2L, K2, rep from * to end.
14th row K1, *T2R, K4, T2L, rep from * to last st, K1.
16th row K8, *T2L, K6, rep from * to last 2 sts, K2.
These 16 rows form the pattern.

Arrowhead honeycomb

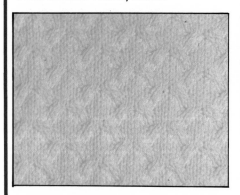

Cast on a multiple of 12 sts plus 2 extra.
1st and every foll alternate row P to end.
2nd row (RS) K to end.
4th row K1, *sl 2 sts onto cable needle (cn) and leave at back of work, K2, then K2 from cn—called cable 4 back or C4B—, K4, sl 2 sts onto cn and leave at front of work, K2, then K2 from cn—called cable 4 front or C4F—, rep from * to last st, K1.
6th row K to end.

8th row K1, *K2, C4F, C4B, K2, rep from * to last st, K1.
These 8 rows form the pattern.

Aran honeycomb circles

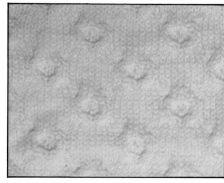

Cast on a multiple of 16 sts plus 2 extra.
1st and every foll alternate row P to end.
2nd row (RS) K to end.
4th row K1, *K8, sl 2 sts onto cable needle (cn) and leave at front of work, K2, then K2 from cn—called cable 4 front or C4F—, sl 2 sts onto cn and leave at back of work, K2, then K2 from cn—called cable 4 back or C4B—, rep from * to last st, K1.
6th row K to end.
8th row K1, *C4B, C4F, K8, rep from * to last st, K1.
10th row K to end.
12th row K1, *C4F, C4B, K8, rep from * to last st, K1.
14th row K to end.
16th row K1, *K8, C4B, C4F, rep from * to last st, K1.
These 16 rows form the pattern.

Herringbone lattice

Cast on a multiple of 8 sts.
1st and every foll alternate row (WS) P to end.
2nd row *T2L, K2, T2L, T2R, rep from *.
4th row K1, *T2L, K2, T2R, K2, rep from * ending last repeat K1.
6th row *T2R, T2L, T2R, K2, rep from *.
8th row K3, *T2L, K2, T2R, K2, rep from * to last 5 sts, T2L, K3.
These 8 rows form the pattern.

Diamond lattice

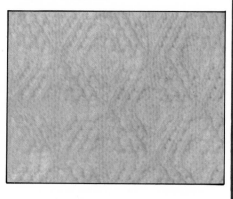

Cast on a multiple of 16 sts plus 1 extra.
1st and every foll alternate row P to end.
2nd row (RS) K1, *(T2L) 3 times, K3, (T2R) 3 times, K1, rep from * to end.
4th row K2, *(T2L) 3 times, K1, (T2R) 3 times, K3, rep from * ending last repeat K2.
6th row As 2nd.
8th row As 4th.
10th row K to end.
12th row K2, *(T2R) 3 times, K1, (T2L) 3 times, K3, rep from * ending last repeat K2.
14th row K1, *(T2R) 3 times, K3, (T2L) 3 times, K1, rep from * to end.
16th row As 12th.
18th row As 14th.
20th row K to end.
These 20 rows form the pattern.

Traveling cables

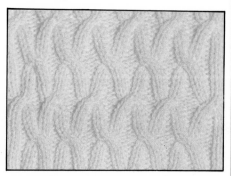

Cast on a multiple of 8 sts plus 2 extra.
1st, 3rd, 5th and 7th rows (WS) K2, *P2, K2, rep from * to end.
2nd, 4th and 6th rows P2, *K2, P2, rep from * to end.
8th row P2, *sl next 4 sts onto cable needle (cn) and leave at back of work, K2, sl 2 purl sts from cn back onto left-hand needle and P them, K2 from cn, P2, rep from * to end.
9th to 15th rows As first to 7th.
16th row P2, K2, *P2, sl next 4 sts onto cn and leave at front of work, K2, sl 2 purl sts from cn back onto left-hand needle and P them, K2 from cn, rep from * to last 6 sts, P2, K2, P2.
These 16 rows form the pattern.

Child's duffle coat

An Aran duffle coat to knit in an allover cable pattern.

Sizes

To fit 22[24:26]in (56[61:66]cm) chest.
Length, 19[21:23]in (48[53:58]cm).
Sleeve seam, 9¾[11:12]in (25[28:31]cm) 31]cm.
Note Directions for larger sizes are in brackets []; if there is only one set of figures it applies to all sizes.

Materials

20[22:25]oz (550[600:700]g) of a
    knitting worsted
1 pair each Nos. 4 and 6 (3¾ and
    4½mm) knitting needles
Cable needle (cn); 3 toggles

Gauge

24 stitches and 28 rows to 4in (10cm) over lattice pattern on No. 6 (4½mm) knitting needles.

Back

Using No. 6 (4½mm) needles cast on 73[79:85] sts.
1st ribbing row K1, (P1, K1) to end.
2nd ribbing row P1, (K1, P1) to end.
Rep these 2 rows once more, inc one st at center of last row. 74[80:86] sts.
Beg patt.
1st row K5, *P2, K4, rep from * to last 3 sts, P2, K1.
2nd row K3, *P4, K2, rep from * to last 5 sts, P4, K1.
3rd row K1, *sl next 2 sts onto cn and leave at front of work, K2, then K2 from cn—called cable 4 front or C4F—, P2, rep from * to last st, K1.
4th row As 2nd.
5th row K1, P2, *K2, sl next 2 sts onto cn and leave at back of work, K2, then P2

from cn—called cable 4 right of C4R—, rep from * to last 5 sts, K5.
6th row K1, *P4, K2, rep from * to last st, K1.
7th row K1, *P2, sl next 2 sts onto cn and leave at back of work, K2, then K2 from cn—called cable 4 back or C4B—, rep from * to last st, K1.
8th row As 6th.
9th row K5, *sl next 2 sts onto cn and leave at front of work, P2, then K2 from cn—called cable 4 left or C4L—, K2, rep from * to last 3 sts, P2, K1.
10th row As 2nd.
Rep 3rd–10th rows until work measures 19[21:23]in (48[53:58]cm); end with a WS row. Bind off.

Pattern panel for fronts (worked on 24 sts).
1st row K2, P8, K4, P8, K2.
2nd row K10, P4, K10.
3rd row K2, P7, sl next st onto cn and leave at back of work, K2, then K1 from

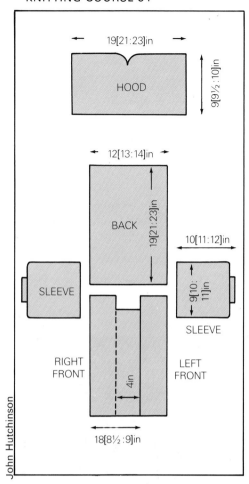

19[21:23]in

HOOD

9[9½:10]in

12[13:14]in

BACK

19[21:23]in

10[11:12]in

SLEEVE

9[10:11]in

SLEEVE

RIGHT
FRONT

LEFT
FRONT

4in

18[8½:9]in

John Hutchinson

22nd row As 8th.

23rd row K2, P5, Cr3F, C4B, Cr3B, P5, K2.

24th row As 6th.

25th row K2, P6, Cr3F, K2, Cr3B, P6, K2.

26th row As 4th.

27th row K2, P7, Cr3F, Cr3B, P7, K2.

28th row As 2nd.

29th row K2, P8, C4F, P8, K2.

30th row As 2nd.

Rep 3rd–30th rows throughout.

Left front

Using No. 6 (4½mm) needles cast on 49[53:55] sts.

1st ribbing row (K1, P1) to last 3 sts, K3.

2nd ribbing row K2, P1, (K1, P1) to end.

Rep these 2 rows once more, inc one st on last row on 1st and 3rd sizes only. 50[53:56] sts.

Beg patt.

1st row K5, (P2, K4) 3[4:4] times, P2[0:2], K1[0:1], then patt 24 sts of panel.

2nd row Patt 24 sts of panel, K3[0:3], (P4, K2) to last 5 sts, P4, K1.

3rd row K1, (C4F, P2) 4[4:5] times, K1 [C4F:K1], then patt 24 sts of panel.

4th row Patt 24 sts of panel, then work as 2nd row.

5th row K1, P2, (K2, C4R) 3[4:4] times, K5[2:5], patt 24.

6th row Patt 24, K1[0:1], P4[2:4], (K2, P4) 3[4:4] times, K3.

7th row K1, (P2, C4B) 4[4:5] times, K1[P2, K1:K1], patt 24.

8th row Patt 24, then work as 6th row.

9th row K5, (C4L, K2) 3[4:4] times, P2, K1[P0:P2, K1], then patt 24.

10th row Patt 24, then work as 2nd row.

Cont as now set, rep 3rd–10th rows for main patt and work the front 24 sts as given for panel, until work measures 17[18½:20]in (43[47:51]cm); with a RS row.

Shape neck

Next row Bind off 24, patt to end. Cont straight until work measures the same as back to shoulders. Bind off.

Right front

Using No. 6 (4½mm) needles cast on 49[53:55] sts.

1st ribbing row K3, (P1, K1) to end.

2nd ribbing row (P1, K1) to last 3 sts, P1, K2. Rep these 2 rows once more, inc one st in last row on 1st and 3rd sizes only. 50[53:56] sts. Beg patt.

1st row Patt 24 sts of panel, K5[2:5], (P2, K4) to last 3 sts, P2, K1.

2nd row K3, (P4, K2) 3[4:4] times, P4[2:4], K1[0:1], patt 24 sts of panel.

3rd row Patt 24 sts of panel, K1[K2, P2: K1], (C4F, P2) to last st, K1.

4th row Patt as 2nd row to last 24 sts, patt 24 sts of panel.

5th row Patt 24, K1, P2[K0:K1, P2], (K2, C4R) to last 5 sts, K5.

6th row K1, (P4, K2) 4[4:5] times, K1[P4:K1], patt 24.

7th row Patt 24, K1 [0:1], P2[0:2], (C4B, P2) to last 5 sts, C4B, K1.

8th row Patt as 6th row to last 24 sts, patt 24.

9th row Patt 24, K5[2:5], (C4L, K2) to last 3 sts, P2, K1.

10th row Patt as 2nd row to last 24 sts, patt 24.

Cont to match left front to neck shaping.

Shape neck

Next row Patt to last 24 sts, bind off these 24 sts. Break off yarn.

Rejoin yarn to rem sts and complete to match left front.

Sleeves

Using No. 4 (3¾mm) needles cast on 37[41:45] sts and work 2 ribbing rows of back 3 times, then work 1st ribbing row again.

Inc row P twice into first st, *K1, P twice into next st, rep from * to end. 56[62:68] sts.

Change to No. 6 (4½mm) needles and cont in patt as for back until work measures 10[11:12]in (25[28:31]cm); end with a WS row. Bind off loosely.

Hood

Using No. 6 (4½mm) needles cast on 114[126:138] sts.

1st row K2, patt as 1st row of back to last 2 sts, K2.

Keeping 2 sts at each end in garter st, cont in patt as for back until work measures 7½[8:8½]in (19[20:21]cm); end with a WS row.

Shape top

Next row Patt 57[63:69], turn and cont on these sts.

Dec one st at inside edge on next and foll 2 alternate rows, then on foll 4[6:8] rows. Bind off. Return to sts that were left and work to match first side.

Pocket

Using No. 6 (4½mm) needles cast on 24[26:28] sts.

1st row P10[11:12], K4, P10[11:12].

2nd row K10[11:12], P4, K10[11:12].

3rd row P9[10:11], Cr3R, Cr3L, P9[10:11].

Keeping the outer sts in reverse stockinette st, work as for front panel until the 28th row has been completed. Change to No. 4 (3¾mm) needles and cont in K1, P1 ribbing beg first row with P1 and inc 5 sts evenly across first row. Rib 4 rows. Bind off in ribbing.

To finish

Do not press. Join shoulder seams. Mark depth of armholes 4½[5:5½]in (11[13:14] cm) from shoulder seams, then sew sleeves to armholes between markers. Join side and sleeve seams. Beg and ending at center of front panels, sew on hood. Sew 3 toggles to one front and make 3 button loops on other front. Sew on pocket.

cn–called cross 3 right or Cr3R–, sl next 2 sts onto cn and leave at front of work, K1, then K2 from cn–called cross 3 left or Cr3L–, P7, K2.

4th row K9, P6, K9.

5th row K2, P6, Cr3R, K2, Cr3L, P6, K2.

6th row K8, P8, K8.

7th row K2, P5, sl next st onto cn and leave at back of work, K2, then P1 from cn–called cross 3 back or Cr3B–, C4B, sl next 2 sts onto cn and leave at front of work, P1, then K2 from cn–called cross 3 front or Cr3F–, P5, K2.

8th row K7, P2, K1, P4, K1, P2, K7.

9th row K2, P4, Cr3B, P1, K4, P1, Cr3F, P4, K2.

10th row K6, P2, K2, P4, K2, P2, K6.

11th row K2, P3, Cr3B, P2, C4B, P2, Cr3F, P3, K2.

12th row K5, P2, K3, P4, K3, P2, K5.

13th row K2, P2, Cr3B, P3, K4, P3, Cr3F, P2, K2.

14th row K4, P2, K4, P4, K4, P2, K4.

15th row K2, P2, P4, C4B, P4, K2, P2, K2.

16th row As 14th.

17th row K2, P2, Cr3F, P3, K4, P3, Cr3B, P2, K2.

18th row As 12th.

19th row K2, P3, Cr3F, P2, C4B, P2, Cr3B, P3, K2.

20th row As 10th.

21st row K2, P4, Cr3F, P1, K4, P1, Cr3B, P4, K2.

Knitting/COURSE 55

Introduction to jacquard knitting

Jacquard is a term for color knitting in which more than two colors are used in a row. The term encompasses many different types of colored patterns including multi-colored motifs, border patterns, allover patterns and collage knitting (this is a name for fabrics with allover irregular or geometric-shaped patches of color). In some cases jacquard patterns may be confused with Fair Isle knitting, the distinction being that true Fair Isle, strictly speaking, uses only two colors across any one row.

Certain techniques are used throughout all forms of color knitting. Carrying or weaving the yarns across the back of the work, as in Fair Isle knitting, is also possible in jacquard patterns. However, with a large number of colors in a row, the carrying method may be too clumsy; many patterns require small, separate balls of yarn for each block of color, with the yarns twisted together at each color change across a row. As with other color patterns, many jacquard designs are worked from a chart with the first few rows written out to set the position.

Most multi-colored designs look best in stockinette stitch, which focuses attention on the colors and design rather than the stitch texture. Jacquard patterns are an ideal way of using up small amounts of yarn in an unusual and creative way.

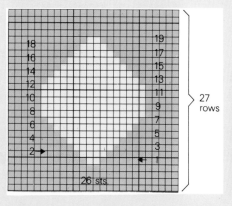

Mike Berend

Jacquard knitting techniques

The correct method of working multi-colored jacquard designs with relatively large blocks of color is to use a small, separate ball of yarn for each color. If you use a color more than once across a row, each section must have its own individual ball of yarn. This method will produce a single-thickness fabric without any strands of yarn across the back. To prevent any holes in the fabric, twist the yarns around each other when changing color, as with wide stripes (see Volume 7, pages 29-30).

Practice these techniques by knitting the shape shown in step 1. When the outline moves diagonally to the right (viewed from the right side) loop the yarns on a knit row but not a purl one, as the purl stitch encroaches into the pattern and automatically loops. With an outline sloping to the left, loop the yarns on a purl row and not on a knit row.

18 16 14 12 10 8 6 4 2

19 17 15 13 11 9 7 5 3 1

27 rows

26 sts.

1 Before knitting a fabric from this chart, wind a small, separate ball of yarn from the main background color (A); for the 1st pattern row, where you join in the 2nd color (B), you will need 2 balls of the main color. Using A, cast on 26 stitches. Work 4 rows stockinette st.

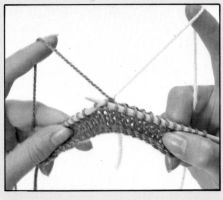

2 Work 1st patt row: using A K12 sts, join in B by loosely knotting at back of next st on left-hand needle, cross (A) right in front of left (above), looping B around A; K2 sts with B, join in a small ball of A to back of last st on right-hand needle, K12 sts with A without looping. *continued*

Brian Mayor

3 The next pattern row is on the wrong side of the fabric: the first side of the shape you reach is sloping one stitch to the left (when viewed from the right side); therefore you must cross the yarns on a WS row. Work 2nd patt row: using small ball of A, K11 sts, cross right yarn (A) in front of left as shown, so looping B around A.

4 Continue row: P4 sts with B, then P11 sts with A. There is no need to loop the yarns when working the last stitches in A; the second side of the shape on a WS row is sloping to the right.

5 Work 3rd patt row: using A K10 sts, cross right yarn (A) in front of left, so looping B around A. It is necessary to loop yarns on this RS row as the side of the shape is sloping to the right.

6 Continue row: K6 sts with B, then K10 sts with small ball of A. There is no need to loop the yarns when working the last stitches in A; the second side of the shape on a RS row is sloping to the left.

7 Work from the chart until the 7th pattern row is complete: follow the order of looping yarns indicated in steps 3 to 6. In rows 8 to 12 the sides of the shape are vertical: you must loop the yarns at the color change in each row.

8 In rows 13 to 19 the sides of the shape are sloping in reverse order—first to the left, then to the right. Therefore, loop the yarns at the end of knit and purl rows but not at the beginning.

Knitting in a simple motif

If you have knitted Fair Isle designs, you will be familiar with working from a chart (see Volume 9, page 45). Charts give a good visual indication of how your work should look and take up much less space than written directions.

Most designs are charted on graph paper, allowing one square for each stitch and one line of squares for each row. Different colors are either coded with symbols or lightly shaded in the appropriate color so that the background grid is clearly visible. Although the principal technique involved here is looping the yarns when changing color, it is also possible to carry yarns over small areas of color. Study each row of the chart before knitting to determine the correct working methods.

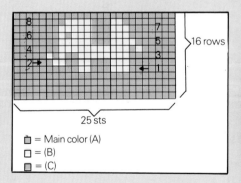

□ = Main color (A)
□ = (B)
□ = (C)

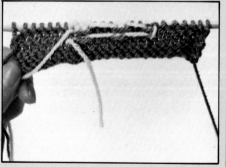

Brian Mayor

1 This elephant motif is knitted into a piece of fabric 25 stitches wide by 16 rows deep. When incorporating a motif into a section of a garment, the pattern sets the 1st row—here it is K7 A, 3 B, 3 A, 2 B, 10 A—so that the motif is in the correct position; thereafter you follow the chart.

2 Before beginning to knit, separate the colors into the number of balls required; in this design only the main color needs dividing. Work the 1st and 2nd pattern rows from the chart, carrying the yarns across the back, as there are only a small number of stitches in each color.

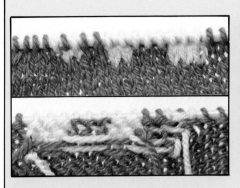
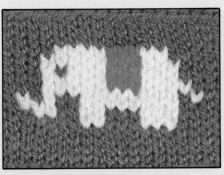

Mike Berend

3 On the 3rd pattern row there are 8 stitches in B across the body of the elephant; this is too many to carry the yarn across. Work 3rd row as follows: Using A, K7, loop yarns (as it is a vertical line), K8 B, join in a small ball of A, loop yarns, K2 A, carry B across, K1 B, 1 A, 1 B and 5 A. The photographs show how the knitting should look on both sides after the 3rd row.

4 Continue working from the chart. Always study the outline of the motif before you begin a row. Consider the direction the lines are sloping, and whether twisting or carrying the yarns would be the better technique.

5 The finished fabric should look very neat on the wrong side. Notice that color B is carried across the 3 saddle stitches in color C: as you work it is apparent that the yarns must be looped as you begin the saddle on each row, but not at the end.

"Pop art" sweaters

Bold motifs transform these classics into works of art.

Sizes
To fit 32[34:36:38:40]in (83[87:92:97: 102]cm) bust/chest.
Length to shoulder, 22[22:23:23:24]in (55[55:57:57:59]cm).
Sleeve seam, 17[17:18:18:19]in (43[43: 46:46:48]cm).
Note Directions for larger sizes are in brackets []; if there is only one set of figures it applies to all sizes.

Materials
15[15:16:17]oz (400[400:425:425: 450]g) of a sport yarn in main shade (A)
1oz (25g) each of contrasting colors (B and C)
1 pair each Nos. 2 and 4 (3 and 3¾mm) knitting needles

Gauge
24 sts and 36 rows to 4in (10cm) in stockinette st on No. 4 (3¾mm) needles.

Lipstick sweater

Back
Using No. 2 (3mm) needles and A, cast on 92[98:104:110:116] sts. Work 2in (5cm) K1, P1 ribbing. Change to No. 4 (3¾mm) needles. Beg with a K row, cont in stockinette st, inc 10 sts evenly across first row. 102[108:114:120:126] sts. Work 112[112:116:116:120] rows stockinette st; end with a P row.
Shape armholes
Bind off 6 sts at beg of next 2 rows.

Next row K1, sl 1, K1, psso, K to last 3 sts, K2 tog, K1.
Next row P to end.
Rep last 2 rows until 78[84:90:96:102] sts rem. Cont straight until 68[68:72:72: 76] rows have been worked from beg of armhole; end with a P row.
Shape shoulders
Bind off 8[9:10:10:11] sts at beg of next 4 rows and 9[9:9:11:11] sts at beg of foll 2 rows. Change to No. 2 (3mm) needles. Work 1in (2.5cm) K1, P1 ribbing on rem 28[30:32:34:36] sts for back neckband; end with a WS row. Bind off

loosely in ribbing.

Front
Work as for back until 20[20:24:24:28] rows have been completed in stockinette st. Beg motif, working from chart.
1st row K32[35:38:41:44] A, 2 B, 68[71:74:77:80] A.
Cont as for back, working from chart, until 46[46:48:52] rows have been worked from beg of armhole; end with a P row.
Shape neck
Next row K29[31:33:35:37], turn and

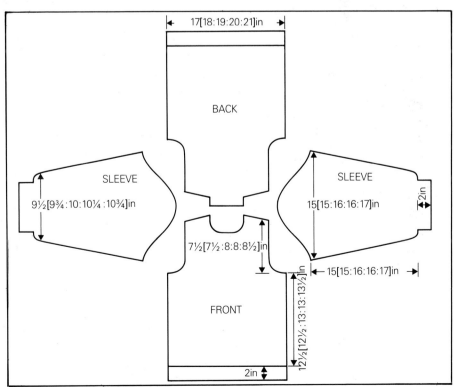

leave rem sts on a spare needle.
Finish left side of neck first. Dec one
st at neck edge on every row until
25[27:29:31:33] sts rem. Cont straight
until 22[22:24:24:24] rows have been
worked from beg of neck; end with a P
row.

Shape shoulder
Bind off 8[9:10:10:11] sts at beg of
next and foll alternate rows. Work 1 row.
Bind off rem 9[9:9:11:11] sts.
With RS of work facing, sl 20[22:24:26:
28] sts at center front neck onto a holder,
rejoin yarn to next st and K to end.
Finish to match first side, reversing
shaping. Using No. 2 (3mm) needles, A
and with RS of work facing, pick up and K
21[21:23:23:23] sts from left side of

neck, K across sts on holder and pick up
and K 21[21:23:23:23] sts up right side
of neck. 62[64:70:72:74] sts. Work
1in (2.5cm) K1, P1 ribbing; end with a
WS row. Bind off loosely in ribbing.

Sleeves
Using No. 2 (3mm) needles and A, cast on
46[48:50:52:54] sts. Work 2in (5cm) K1,
P1 ribbing. Change to No. 4 (3¾mm)
needles. Beg with a K row, cont in
stockinette st, inc 10 sts evenly across
first row. 56[58:60:62:64] sts. Work 2
rows. Inc one st at each end of next and
every foll 8th row until there are
90[90:96:96:102] sts. Cont straight
until sleeve measures 17[17:18:18:19]in
(43[43:46:46:48]cm); end with a P row.

Shape top
Bind off 6 sts at beg of next 2 rows.
Next row K1, sl 1, K1, psso, K to last 3
sts, K2 tog, K1.
Next row P to end. Rep last 2 rows until
48[50:52:54:56] sts rem.
Next row K1, sl 1, K1, psso, K to last
3 sts, K2 tog, K1.
Next row P1, P2 tog, P to last 3 sts, P2
tog tbl, P1.
Rep last 2 rows until 24[22:24:22:24]
sts rem. Bind off.

To finish
Press or block according to yarn used.
Join shoulders. Set in sleeves. Join side
and sleeve seams. Duplicate stitch
outlines in A shown as crosses on chart
(see Volume 1, page 38).

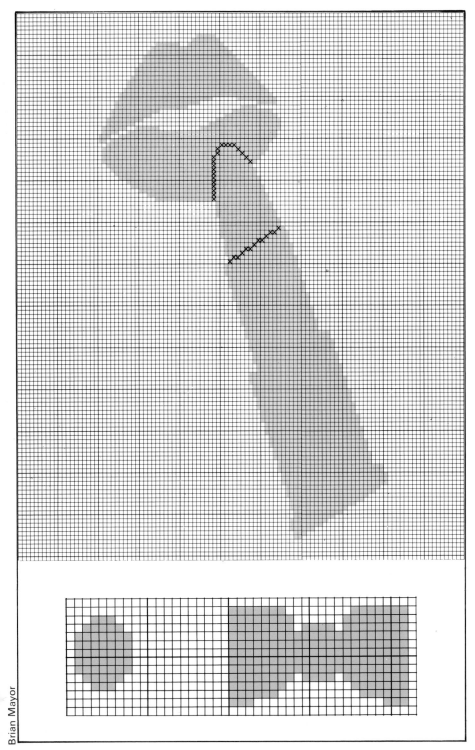

Brian Mayor

Bow tie sweater

Back
Work as for lipstick sweater back.

Front
Work as for back until 56[56:60:60:64] rows have been completed in stockinette st. Beg motif, following chart.
1st row K54[57:60:63:66] A, 3 B, K45[48:51:54:57] A.
Cont following chart until 9 rows of button motif are complete. Cont in stockinette st, working 96[96:100:100:

104] rows; end with a P row. Beg shirt front.
Next row K50[53:56:59:62] A, 2 C, K to end with A.
Next row P50[53:56:59:62] A, 2 C, P to end with A.
Rep last 2 rows once more.
Next row K49[52:55:58:61] A, 4 C, K to end with A.
Next row P49[52:55:58:61] A, 4 C, P to end with A.
Rep last 2 rows once more. Cont in this way, working 2 more sts in C on next and every foll 4th row, until 112[112:116:

116:120] rows stockinette st have been worked; end with a P row.
Shape armholes
Cont to work shirt front as before, *at the same time* shape armholes as given for back until 34[34:36:36:40] rows have been worked from beg of armhole shaping. 26[26:26:26:28] sts in C.
Beg bow tie motif, following chart and shaping shirt front as before.
1st row Patt 28[31:34:37:40] sts, 3 B, 16 C, 3 B, patt to end.
Cont to shape shirt front until 25[27:29:31:33] sts rem in A on each side, *at the same time* work 12 rows of bow tie from chart.
Keeping relevant sts in A and C when shaping neck, complete as given for lipstick sweater front from neck shaping to end.

Sleeves
Work as for lipstick sweater sleeves.

Left lapel
Using No. 4 (3¾mm) needles and A, cast on 2 sts.
1st row K to end.
2nd row P to end.
3rd row K twice into first st, K1.
4th row Sl 1, K1, psso, K1.
5th row As 3rd.
6th row P to end.
7th row K twice into first st, K to last 2 sts, K2 tog.
8th row P to end.
9th row K twice into first st, K to end.
10th row P to end.
Rep 7th-10th rows until there are 13 sts, ending with a 10th row.
Next row Sl 1, K1, psso, K to last 2 sts, K2 tog.
Next row P to last 2 sts, P2 tog tbl.
Next row Sl 1, K1, psso, K to end.
Next row P to last 2 sts, P2 tog tbl.
Next row Cast on 8 sts, K to last 2 sts, K2 tog.
Work 3 rows stockinette st.
Next row K to last 2 sts, K 2 tog.
Work 3 rows stockinette st. Rep last 4 rows until 13[12:11:10:9] sts rem. Cont in stockinette st without shaping until lapel matches edge of shirt front; end with a WS row. Bind off.

Right lapel
Work as for left lapel, reversing shaping.

To finish
Press or block, according to yarn used. Sew lapels to front, joining inside edge to edge of shirt front and leaving outer edge unattached. Join shoulder seams, including top edge of lapel. Using B, embroider a vertical line of chain stitch on left side of button to represent front opening of jacket. Using a small crochet hook and B, work 1 row of single crochet around lapel edges. Set in sleeves. Join side and sleeve seams.

*Overlaid cuff
*Boned plackets
*Conspicuous placket
 opening with hook and
 eye fastening
*Pattern for a sweetheart
 dress (1):
 adapting the pattern

Overlaid cuff

When a cuff with an unusual shape is applied to a full sleeve, as on the dress on page 65, it is unnecessary to cut the sleeve to the same shape as the cuff if you use an overlaid seam construction. The cuff is cut in one piece and overlaid on the sleeve, enclosing all the raw edges. This method can be adapted for use with other hem edges such as wrists, blouses gathered into a band at the waist or hips, pants or pedal pushers with shaped knee or ankle cuffs, or on shorts with overlaid cuffs at the legs. Here the cuff has a pointed shape, but another shape, such as scallops or curves, could look just as good, and the technique remains the same.

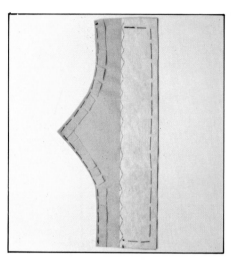

1 Baste the interfacing to the wrong side of the cuff and catch-stitch it to the foldline. Turn under a ⅝in (1.5cm) seam allowance along the shaped edge and baste. Press flat and clip into the seam allowance on shaped edges where necessary.

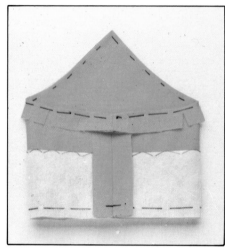

2 Reduce the sleeve fullness at the lower edge and complete the underarm seam. Remove basting near short ends along shaped edge. Join the cuff seam with right sides together, and raw edges even. Baste and stitch along seam allowance. Baste and press shaped edge as before.

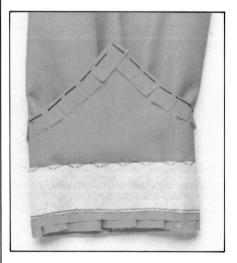

3 Slip cuff over sleeve with seams and raw edges matching and with the point of the cuff toward the sleeve cap. The right side of the cuff is applied to the wrong side of the sleeve. Baste and stitch seam. Grade the seam as shown and press well on the seamline only. Do not press the gathered part of the sleeve.

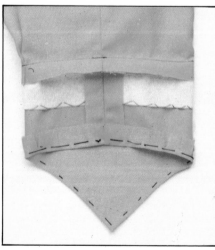

4 Pull the cuff down through the sleeve and press the seam flat toward the cuff edge. Trim away excess fabric where seams cross.

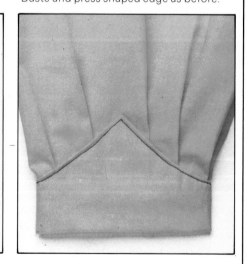

5 Turn the cuff upward, pressing along the foldline, and position carefully on the sleeve, adjusting basting so that the cuff lies flat. Baste and stitch in place close to the shaped edge as for an overlaid seam. Remove basting and press.

Boned plackets

Boning a garment can give it shape or support. Originally boning was made of whalebone and later of sprung metal; today it is made of washable polyester and can be stitched in place without a separate casing. The dress bodice on page 65 has boning inserted into plackets so that it is removable.

The topstitching is easiest to do using a zipper foot on the machine. Or you can sew topstitching by hand, using backstitch.

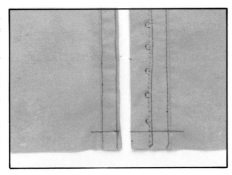

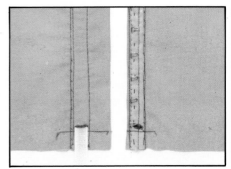

1 After applying the placket pieces to the garment as shown below, sew two rows of topstitching from the right side of the garment down the center of each piece, making the space between each row ⅛in (3mm) wider than the boning used. Stitch across the bottom of each placket piece at waist seamline to prevent boning from slipping out.

2 Make a small horizontal buttonhole by hand on the inside of the placket pieces immediately above the waistline and between the two rows of topstitching. Insert the boning through each of the holes and trim to size. Close the holes with slip stitching.

Conspicuous placket opening with hook and eye fastening

Plackets with hooks and eyes are a traditional method of fastening a garment and can be decorative as well as strong. When this kind of fastening is put into a faced edge, such as on the bodice of the dress on page 65, the placket pieces are stitched to the bodice edges after the neck fastenings have been applied. In this case the first and third foldlines on the left placket pattern mark the center front but could instead mark the center back or side seam; the principle remains the same.

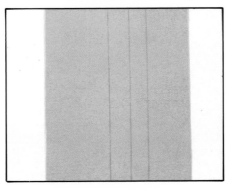

1 To make the left side of placket, transfer the foldline (shown at left) and center front positions from the pattern to the placket piece with tailor's chalk or basting.

2 Fold the placket with wrong sides together along the first center front line and baste ⅛in (3mm) from the fold. Press.

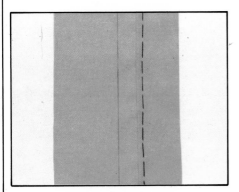

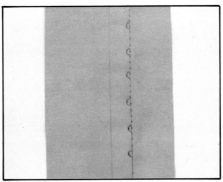

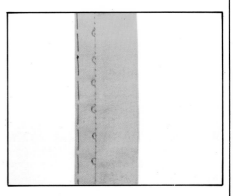

3 Fold the placket again, right sides together, to match the center front lines, so that a tiny pleat is formed on the wrong side of the placket. Baste in place, through all thicknesses, close to folded edge. Remove previous basting.

4 The eyes are positioned ½in (1.2cm) apart, the first eye being ¾in (2cm) from placket top. On right side, slip stitch eyes into small pleat between the two center fronts, stitching these together and securing the eyes. Remove basting.

5 Fold the placket along the placket foldline with wrong sides together and press. Remove basting from pleat section only.

continued

Simon Butcher

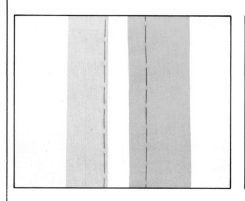

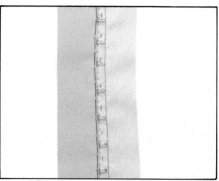

6 To make the right placket, turn under the ⅝in (1.5cm) seam allowance along the center front edge of one placket piece. Baste close to folded edge. Mark the center front on the other with a row of basting. (Contrasting fabrics are used here for clarity.)

7 Lay the folded piece over the flat section with wrong sides together. The basted center front edge should lie slightly away from the folded edge so that when the hooks are in place they will not show from the right side. Position the hooks to correspond with eyes, slip stitching them down between the two placket pieces. Topstitch close to hooks.

8 Fold the other placket piece back on the center front line, trimming off the raw edge of one piece to match the other. Press. Do not remove basting. The plackets are now ready to apply to the garment; since the placket has been trimmed, it will be necessary to take a narrower seam when applying the placket.

Sweetheart dress (1)

A pretty dress with its own coordinating jacket is perfect for late summer days.

Adapting the pattern

Measurements

The dress is made by adapting the pattern for the basic dress and the basic shirt from the Stitch by Stitch Pattern Pack, available in sizes 10-20, corresponding to sizes 8-18 in ready-made clothes. This course gives directions for adapting the pattern; directions for making the dress are on page 70. For the jacket adaptation, see Volume 11, page 77.

Materials

5 sheets of tracing paper 36×40in (approx 90×100cm)
Yardstick
Flexible curve
Tailor's square

Note: The dress shown here has a decorative front placket with a hook and eye fastening, but since there is a zipped opening at the center back, the dress front could be stitched flat, with buttons added for effect only.

Bodice

1 Trace the top part of the dress front pattern down to a few inches (centimeters) below waist level. Mark in the side bust dart and the waist dart.

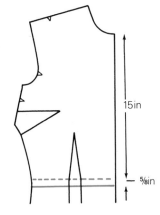

2 To mark the waist seam, measure down the center front edge from the front neck cutting line 15in (38cm) for a size 10, adding an extra ¼in (6mm) to this measurement for each larger size.
3 Draw a line across the pattern at right angles to the center front at this point. Add a ⅝in (1.5cm) seam allowance and cut the pattern along this line.

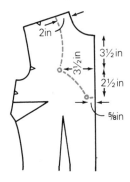

4 To shape the new neckline, measure 3½in (9cm) down the center front edge,

from front neck cutting line and draw a line across the pattern at right angles to it. Mark a point 3½in (9cm) along this line with a circle.

5 Measure down the center front edge a further 2½in (6.5cm) and mark. Measure in ⅝in (1.5cm) from this point and mark with a circle. At the shoulder measure along the shoulderline from the neck cutting line 2in (5cm) and mark.

6 Using a flexible curve, start at the shoulder seamline and draw a curve to the first circle then another curve to the circle at the center front seamline. The downward curve will be very slight, but the curve across to the front edge will be rounder.

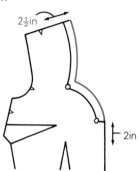

7 Add ⅝in (1.5cm) seam allowance to curved edges of the new neckline and cut around the new neck cutting line. To cut the front neck facing pattern, measure 2½in (6.5cm) out along the shoulder cutting line and 2in (5cm) down center front edge from circle. Trace new neckline, shoulder and center front edges, marking circles and seam allowances.

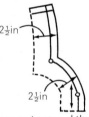

8 Measure out around the neck cutting line at 2½in (6.5cm) intervals, which will be the outline of the facing shape. Cut along this line for the facing pattern.

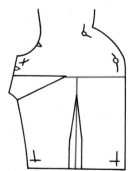

9 For the front shaping, the bust dart and waist dart allowance are transferred to the front edge. Continue the top line of the bust dart to the center front edge. Draw

a line to meet this, through the middle of waist dart and parallel to center front.

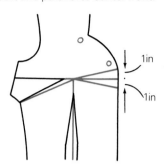

10 From the lower bust dart at the side edge, draw a line to meet the point where the lines cross. At the center front edge measure 1in (2.5cm) from each side of extended bust dart line and mark. Draw a line from each mark to the point where the other lines intersect.

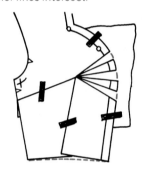

11 Cut along the three lines from the front edge to the new dart point. Cut through the center line of the waist dart as far as the new dart point. Lay the front edge of the pattern over a piece of paper ready to tape in place.

12 Close the side bust dart and tape in place. Overlap the waist dart stitching lines until they are aligned. Tape in place. The pattern will now be open at the front edge. Spread each slash by equal amounts and tape down. Smooth lower line.

13 Redraw the cutting line over the front curved edge. Mark all the seam allowances. Mark in the grain line parallel to the center front edge.

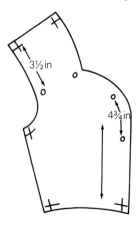

14 To mark the point where the sleeve gathering position matches at the arm,

measure down the armhole seamline from the shoulder seamline 3½in (9cm) for size 10, adding an extra ¼in (6mm) for each larger size. Mark with a circle.

15 To mark the tucking allowance, measure 4¾in (12cm) down from the circle at center front and mark with a circle. Tuck between the two circles.

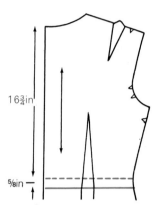

16 To make the back pattern, trace the upper section of the dress back pattern to a few inches (centimeters) below waist level. Mark grain line and the waist and shoulder darts, and indicate that the center back is placed on the fold.

17 To mark waist seam, measure down center back from back neck cutting line 16¾in (42.5cm) for size 10, adding an extra ¼in (6mm) for each larger size. Draw a line across pattern from this point perpendicular to center back. Add ⅝in (1.5cm) for seam. Cut pattern along waistline.

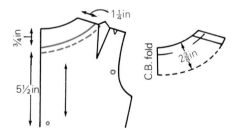

18 For the neck curve, measure ¾in (2cm) down center back from the back neck cutting line and mark. Measure 1¼in (3cm) along shoulder seamline from neck cutting line and mark. Using a flexible curve, connect these two points to form new back neck curve. Mark a ⅝in (1.5cm) seam allowance below new neckline.

19 To mark top of zipper opening, measure 5½in (14cm) down the center back seamline from the new neck seamline and mark with a circle. The sleeve gathering position will be the same as for front; mark it with another circle.

20 To cut the back neck facing, trace the new back neck cutting line, the center back seamline and the shoulder cutting line. The center back will be placed on a fold. Mark line at 2⅜in (6cm) depth from neck cutting line. Mark in the seam allowance. The grain line will be parallel to the center back.

Sleeve

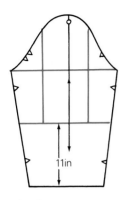

11in

1 To make the sleeve pattern, trace the dress sleeve pattern and mark the grain line. For the sleeve length, measure up from lower edge of sleeve 11in (28cm). Draw a line across the pattern at this point perpendicular to the grain line. This measurement includes a ⅝in (1.5cm) seam allowance. Cut along this line.

2 Extend the grain line to the top of the sleeve cap. Draw a horizontal line across the pattern between the underarm points. Divide this line into four equal sections; draw two vertical lines, parallel to the grain line, through the intermediate points.

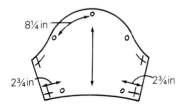

2½in   2in   2½in
2½in
1⅝in   2⅜in   1⅝in

3 Before cutting the pattern, lay it over a piece of paper so that it can be taped in place immediately. Cut through all the vertical lines and, using the horizontal line as a guide to keep pattern balanced, spread pattern out with equal spaces of 2½in (6.5cm) at top edge.

4 Spread out lower edge 1⅝in (4cm) at each side and 2⅜in (6cm) in center. Tape in place. Re-draw the sleeve cap, making it 2in (5cm) higher than original cutting line at center point. Mark ⅝in (1.5cm) seam allowance around the sleeve cap.

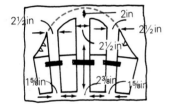

8¼ in

2¾ in   2¾ in

5 For the gathering positions, measure around each side of the sleeve cap along seamline 8¼in (21cm) from center and mark with a circle. For the tucked area at the lower edge, measure along the seamline 2¾in (7cm) from the side cutting lines and mark with circles. Mark grain line through center of sleeve.

Plackets, cuff and belt

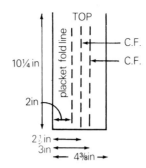

TOP
10¼ in   placket fold line   C.F.   C.F.
2in
2½ in
3in
4⅜ in

1 To make the left front placket piece draw a rectangle 10¼in (26cm) long by 4⅜in (11cm) wide, adding an extra ¼in (6mm) to length only for each larger size. Mark ⅝in (1.5cm) seam allowance which has been included around all edges.

2 Mark a series of parallel lines over the width, at 2in (5cm), 2½in (6.5cm), and 3in (7.5cm) from cutting line. The first foldline is the placket facing. The second and third lines mark the center front. The grain runs parallel to these lines.

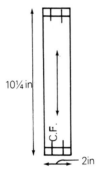

10¼ in
C.F.
2in

3 To make right front placket piece draw a rectangle 10¼in (26cm) long by 2in (5cm) wide for size 10, adding an extra ¼in (6mm) to length for each larger size. Mark ⅝in (1.5cm) seam allowances, which have been included around all edges. One of the long seamlines will mark the center front. Mark grain line parallel to center front.

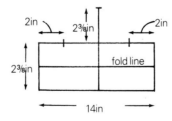

2in   2⅜in   2in
2⅜in   fold line
14in

4 To make cuff pattern, draw a rectangle 14in (35.5cm) long by 2⅜in (6cm) wide adding an extra ⅜in (1cm) to length for each larger size. Draw a horizontal line through center of rectangle. This is the foldline. Draw vertical line through center of rectangle, extending it up by 2⅜in (6cm). On top edge, measure in 2in (5cm) from each side and mark.

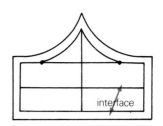

interface

5 Using a flexible curve, draw the curves of the outer point from the center line to these marks. Do not make the curves too deep. Add ⅝in (1.5cm) seam allowance all around cuff. Use the center vertical line as the grain line.

6 To make the tie belt, draw a rectangle 39⅜in (100cm) by 3¾in (7cm) for all sizes. This measurement includes seam allowances of ⅝in (1.5cm) all around.

Skirt

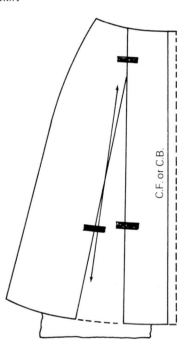

C.F. or C.B.

John Hutchinson

1 To make the skirt pattern, use the basic skirt. Trace the skirt front and back and mark the waist darts. For the front, draw a line through the center of the waist dart and continue the line down to the hemline. Cut up along the marked line as far as the dart point.

2 Close the dart top by matching the dart lines together and tape in place. This will open the skirt. Place paper behind the slash and tape in place. Add ⅝in (1.5cm) seam allowance to center front edge.

3 To mark the grain line, measure along the waistline and the lower edge and mark the center point of each. The line joining the two is the grain line.

4 To make the back, trace the basic skirt back and make the same alterations to the pattern as those given for the skirt front. Add ⅝in (1.5cm) seam allowances to center back edge. Directions for making the dress are on page 70.

*Fabric flowers
*Pattern for a sweetheart
 dress (2):
   directions for making

Fabric flowers

Artificial flowers are fun and make an exotic accessory to a simple garment. They can be made from almost any fabric scraps to contrast with or match your outfit. The poppy on the dress shown on page 71 was made of stiffened flower shapes cut from flower-printed fabric, but you can use any of these methods.

Beginners will find it easiest to use very lightweight, closely woven fabrics and fine milliner's wire (colored white or black) or fine copper wire. Make one or two experimental flowers using the trace patterns given. When you have mastered these techniques, try other shapes and methods.

Taffeta flower

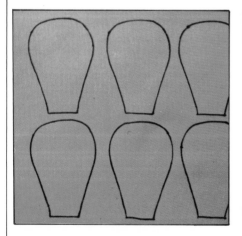

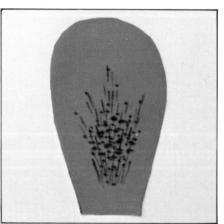

1 Decide how many petals you want for each flower shape and choose the most suitable color and fabric. Mark a series of petal shapes on the fabric. Spray the fabric with stiffener or spray glue to prevent the edges from raveling.

2 If the flowers are to be shaded or marked, make the markings with waterproof ink or paint before cutting out. Gather up the base of the first petal around the stamen. If you cannot buy stamens, use small artificial flowers, or a bead or button attached to the end of a wire stem. Sew securely in place.

3 Repeat with the rest of the petals until a flower shape is formed. Secure the base with thread wound around the stem and sewn securely in place, or use fine milliner's wire.

Chiffon flower

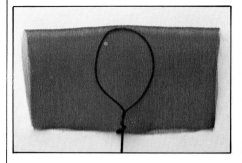

1 Make a frame and stem from fine milliner's wire and cut out a rectangle or circle of fabric large enough to cover the petal frame.

2 Pull the fabric taut around the wire and anchor it at the base with firm stitches. If the petal wire is to be shaped further, work a row of tiny running stitches through fabric close to wire. Use matching thread so stitches are invisible.

3 Secure the first petal to the stamens and twist the stem around the base of the stamens, trimming off excess wire. Make enough petals this way to form the flower. Finish the base of the flower by binding with fine wire or thread.

Stylized flower

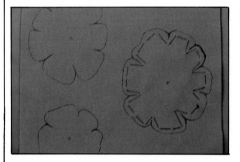

1 With wrong sides together, pin the main fabric and contrasting lining fabric together. Trace the flower shapes on the main fabric. Baste around the shapes just inside the pattern line to hold the fabrics together.

2 Set the machine to a narrow satin stitch or close zig-zag stitch and carefully stitch the shapes following the pattern outlines. Make a tiny buttonhole in the center of each shape. Cut out the shapes close to the stitching.

3 Spray each shape with starch or fabric stiffener and pleat slightly, securing the pleats with small stitches. Put the three shapes together, graduating the sizes, and push a stamen and stem through the holes. Anchor securely.

Bias-strip rose

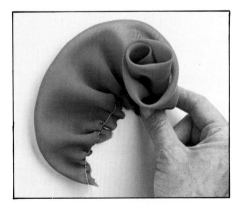

Cut a bias strip 4 × 18in (10 × 46cm) — less for a rosebud. Fold in half lengthwise and fold in ends to make a small curve. Sew a line of running stitches along raw edges through both thicknesses of fabric and gather. Coil fabric and secure threads neatly.

Sweetheart dress (2)

Make it with contrasting trim or a pretty buttoned front.

Directions for making

Suggested fabrics
Lightweight cottons without nap.

Materials
45in (115cm)-wide fabric without
  nap:
  Sizes 10 to 16: 3½yd (3.2m)
  Sizes 18 to 20: 3¾yd (3.4m)
For dress with contrasting pieces:
  45in (115cm)-wide fabric:
  Sizes 10, 12: 3⅓yd (3m)
  Sizes 14, 16: 3½yd (3.2m)
  Sizes 18, 20: 3¾yd (3.4m)
For contrasting pieces:
  45in (115cm)-wide fabric:
  For all sizes: ⅝yd (.5m)
Non-woven interfacing, 36in (90cm)-
  wide for all sizes: ⅝yd (.5m)
Matching thread, 18 hooks and eyes
⅞yd (75cm) polyester boning ⅜in
  (1cm)-wide
18in (46cm) zipper, 7 buttons

Key to adjusted pattern pieces

A	Back bodice	Cut 2
B	Front bodice	Cut 2
C	Front neck facing	Cut 2
D	Back neck facing	Cut 1 on fold
E	Sleeve	Cut 2
F	Cuff	Cut 2
G	Left front placket	Cut 2
H	Right front placket	Cut 2
I	Skirt front	Cut 2
J	Skirt back	Cut 2
K	Belt	Cut 2
Interfacing	Use pieces D,	Cut 1 on fold
	F cut to half width only,	
	and C	Cut 2

1 Prepare the fabric and cut out the pattern pieces. Complete all markings before removing the pattern pieces. Either cut plackets and cuffs in contrasting fabric (see page 65), or make in self fabric, omit boning from placket, stitch together and trim with buttons, as shown here.

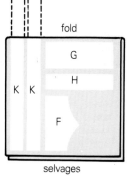

2 With right sides together, baste and stitch the back darts, pressing them toward the center back. With right sides together, baste and stitch the center back seam from neck edge to circle. Press seam open.

Cutting layout for 45in-wide fabric without nap

selvages

J   A   cut 1
    D
  B   K
I
  F   E
G H C

selvages

double thickness

45in-wide fabric without nap (for dress with contrast trim)

selvages

J   A   cut 1
    D
  B
I   E
C

selvages

36in-wide non-woven interfacing

fold

D
  F
C

45in-wide contrast fabric without nap

fold

  G
  H
K K
  F

selvages

John Hutchinson

Victor Yuan

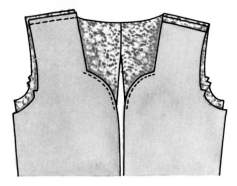

3 Staystitch the curved, front neck edge of the dress bodice. With right sides together, baste and stitch the front and back bodice together at the shoulder seams. Press seams open.

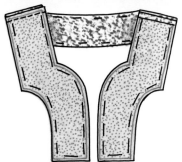

4 Staystitch the inner corners and the curved neck edge of the facings. Baste the interfacing to the wrong side of the front and back neck facings. With right sides together, baste and stitch the facings together at the shoulder seams. Press the seams open.

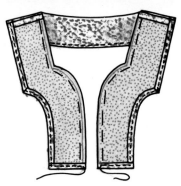

5 Finish the outer edge of the facings by folding under ¼in (6mm) and machine stitching, or by overcasting together. Press the seam allowances flat so they do not show on the right side.

6 With right sides together and shoulder seams and neck edges even, baste and stitch the facing to the neck edge, stitching only as far as the circles at the front edges.

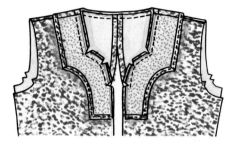

7 Trim the interfacing close to the stitching, grade the seam allowances and clip the neck curves. Clip the seam allowances at the inner corners to the staystitching and to circles as shown.

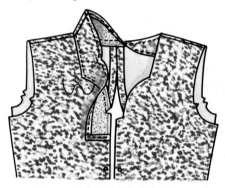

8 Press the seam allowances toward the facing and understitch the facing to the seam allowances. Press. Turn the facing to the inside and baste close to the neck edge. Catch-stitch the facing to the shoulder seams.

9 At the front edges of the bodice, pleat the fullness to fit the placket. Working from the right side of the garment, remove the fullness between the two circles at the front edges of the bodice by forming small tucks in a downward direction. Baste firmly in place. The bodice center front should be the same length as the placket when seamlines are matched.

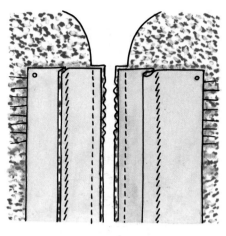

10 Open out both placket pieces without removing lines of marker basting. With right sides together, taking ⅝in (1.5cm) seams, baste and stitch the left front placket piece to the left front, keeping the placket piece free. Baste and stitch the right piece to the right front, keeping the back of the placket piece free. Trim the seam; press.

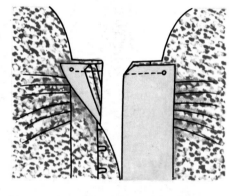

11 Press each placket piece away from the bodice section at the seamline, then back toward the bodice, folding on the marked lines. Baste and stitch across the top edges, as far as the placket seam only. Trim seam allowances and cut across the corners.

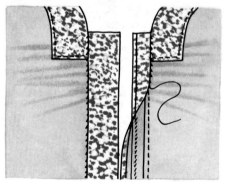

12 Turn the placket pieces right side out at the top edge and press. On the inside, turn under ⅝in (1.5cm) seam allowance of free edge of each placket piece and slip stitch to seamlines. Press. Complete the topstitching and boning (see page 63).

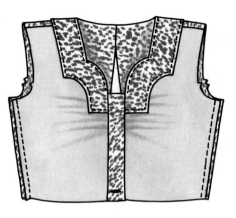

13 With right sides together, baste and stitch the side seams of the bodice sections. Press seams open. Press bodice and facing sections carefully from the wrong side.

14 Run two rows of gathering stitches around the sleeve cap between the gathering positions. Prepare the lower edge of the sleeve by folding the fullness into small even tucks between the circles. The lower edge of the sleeve should be the same measurement as the straight edge of the cuff when seamlines are matched.

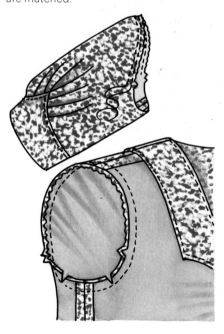

15 Baste and stitch the underarm seam of the sleeve using ⅝in (1.5cm) seam allowance. Complete and attach the cuff (see page 62).

16 With right sides together and seams, shoulder points and circles matching, pin the sleeves into the armholes, pulling up the gathering threads to fit. Spread the gathers evenly over the sleeve caps and baste. Stitch the armhole seams. Clip the circles, trim seam allowances and overcast the edges together. Press the seam allowances into the sleeve caps.

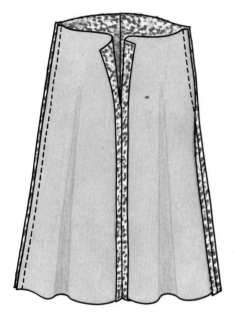

17 With right sides together, baste and stitch the center front seam, the center back and the side seams of the skirt, leaving 8¼in (21cm) at the top of the center back seam for the zipper. Press all seams open.

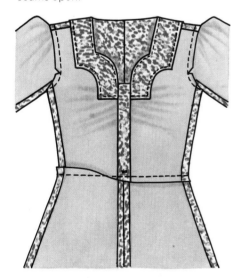

18 Fasten the plackets at the waistline and baste across the bottom of the plackets along the seamline. With right sides together and center backs, side seams and center fronts matching, pin and baste bodice to the skirt around the waist edge. It may be necessary to ease back bodice onto skirt. Stitch waist seam and overcast seam allowances together. Press seam toward bodice.

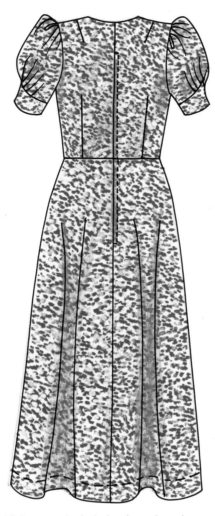

19 Baste and stitch the zipper into the center back opening as for a lapped zipper opening (see Volume 2, page 45). Try on the dress and mark the hemline. Turn up hemline and baste close to fold.

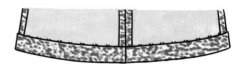

20 Finish the hem edge by turning under a ¼in (6mm) fold and machine stitching. Press. Sew the hem with invisible hemming stitches. Remove basting. Press on folded edge only.

21 With right sides together, baste and stitch the two belt pieces together. Press the seam open. Try the belt on, tying a bow. Trim off excess length at each end if necessary. Then with right sides together, fold the belt in half along its length.

22 Baste and stitch ⅝in (1.5cm) in from raw edges, stitching across ends and along long edge, leaving about 6in (15cm) open in the center. Cut across corners and grade seam allowances. Press.

23 Turn the belt right side out through the opening. Baste around all the outer edges. At the opening, turn in the seam allowance and slip stitch the edges together to close the opening. Press. Make thread belt carriers at side seams of dress on waistline (see Volume 7, page 66).

Terry Evans

Victor Yuan

*Conspicuous zipper in
  a pocket
*Strap seams
*Pattern for a jumpsuit (1):
  adapting the pattern

Conspicuous zipper in a pocket

Zippers are usually concealed by a flap of fabric so that the teeth do not show from the right side. A conspicuous zipper is one where the teeth are exposed to give emphasis to the line of a garment or as a fashion detail. The jumpsuit on page 76 has a conspicuous front zipper and matching zippers on the pockets.

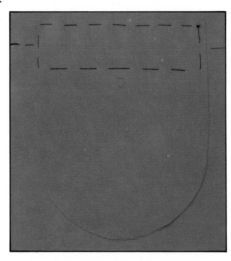

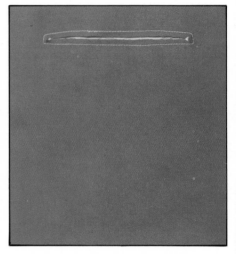

1 Transfer the pocket marking to the garment pieces with tailor's chalk or a basting line. With right sides together, baste one pocket section to the garment, overlapping the top edge of the pocket ¾in (2cm) above the center of the opening.

2 Working from right side of garment, stitch ⅛in (3mm) away from pocket opening all around, using a small stitch. Begin stitching at the center of one side and turn the corners leaving the needle in the fabric. Press and remove basting. Cut through center of opening to within ¼in (6mm) of each end, then diagonally into corners. Do not cut the stitching.

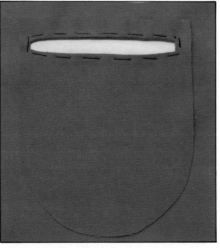

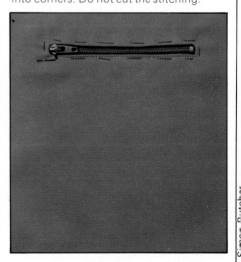

3 Pull the pocket section through the opening to the wrong side and carefully pull out the triangular pieces at each end of the opening.

4 Press the ends and the seam allowances away from the opening and baste all around it. The opening should be about 4in (10cm) long and wide enough that the teeth of the zipper will be exposed when it is inserted.

5 Baste the zipper to the inside of the opening with the teeth showing on the right side, and the zipper tab away from the center when the zipper is closed. Using a zipper foot and working from the right side, stitch along lower edge of the zipper only, stitching close to teeth.

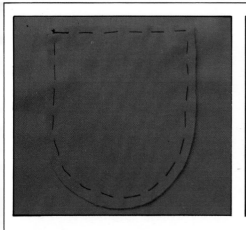

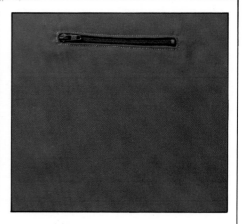

6 Working from the inside of the garment, with right sides together and edges even, baste the second pocket section over the first pocket section. Do not stitch through to the main garment.

7 Stitch the two pocket sections together, stitching from the top, down the side edge and across the bottom and return to the top. Finish the outer edges of the pocket by overcasting them together.

8 On the right side, finish stitching the zipper in place by stitching across one end, along the top edge of the zipper and across the other end, stitching through all thicknesses. This holds the top edge of pocket down. Press. Remove basting.

Strap seams

Strap seams are made from a combination of a plain seam pressed open and a strap of fabric stitched over it on the right side. The strap can be of self-fabric for a subtle effect, or of a contrasting fabric or texture for more visual impact. Materials which do not ravel, such as suede or leather, are easy to apply as they do not need seam allowances. The strap can be narrow or wide, padded, or left flat, as on the jumpsuit on page 76.

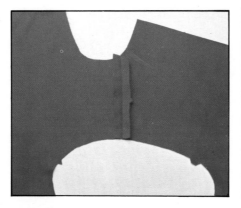

1 Join the front bodice section to the back bodice section at the shoulders. Baste and stitch, taking $\frac{5}{8}$in (1.5cm) seam allowances. Press seams open.

2 Mark the center positioning lines on the sleeve sections with a row of long basting stitches. The top of this line will match the shoulder points.

3 Cut out the strap sections, turn in the seam allowances along the side edges of the strap, baste in place. The seam allowances on these straps are $\frac{5}{8}$in (1.5cm) wide. Press flat.

4 Starting at the neck edge and with the wrong side of the strap to the right side of the garment, center the strap over the shoulder seam and the marked center line of the sleeve and pin in place. Baste along both edges.

5 Stitch the strap in place, stitching close to the basting edges of the strap. Remove all basting and press well.

Susan McLeod

Jumpsuit (1)

This sporty outfit looks great and is practical and hardwearing. Make it in rainproof fabric or, for real luxury, in a soft leather-like fabric.

Measurements

This jumpsuit is made by adapting the pattern for basic shirt and pants from Stitch by Stitch Pattern Pack, available in sizes 10-20, corresponding to 8-18 in ready-made clothes. Directions for adapting the pattern follow; sewing directions are on page 81.

Adapting the pattern

Materials

4 sheets of tracing paper 36 × 40in
(approx 90 × 100cm)
Yardstick
Flexible curve; right triangle

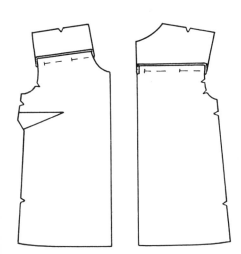

1 To make the back bodice sections, pin the front yoke to the shirt front and the back yoke to the shirt back, aligning the seams. Trace both complete pieces, front and back, leaving extra paper at the center back edge for the pleat.
2 To mark the bodice length on the back pattern, measure down the center back from the neck cutting line 20in (50.5cm) for a size 10, adding an extra ¼in (5mm) for each larger size. This measurement includes a 2in (5cm) allowance for blousing at the waist and a ⅝in (1.5cm) hem allowance at the lower edge.
3 Draw a line across the pattern at this point at a right angle to the center back. To allow for the pleat and the back seam allowance, add 2⅛in (5.5cm) all along the center back edge.

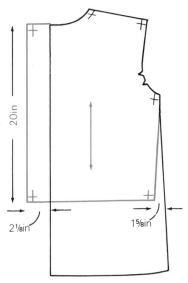

4 Measure in 1⅝in (4cm) from the side seam cutting line along the new waist cutting line. Draw the new side cutting line from the armhole to this point. Mark the grain line parallel to the center back. Mark the seam allowances.

5 To make the back pleat underlay pattern, draw a rectangle the same length as the new center back of the bodice including seam allowances. Make the rectangle 4⅜in (11cm) wide. These measurements include ⅝in (1.5cm) seam allowances on all edges. Draw a line through the center of the rectangle, for the center back and grain line.
6 To mark stitching positions along the center back line, measure up from the lower edge 5in (12.5cm) and down from the top edge 2½in (6.5cm). Mark each point with a circle.
7 To mark the front bodice length, measure down the center front edge from the neck cutting line 18½in (47cm) for a size 10, adding ¼in (5mm) extra for each larger size. Draw a line across pattern at this point at a right angle to center front. This will be the new waist cutting line. A ⅝in (1.5cm) seam has been included.

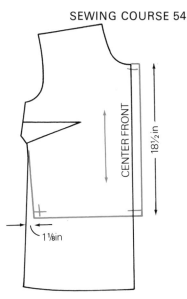

8 Add ⅝in (1.5cm) seam allowance to front edge. Measure in from the side seam cutting line along the new waist cutting line 1⅛in (3cm) and draw in the new side seam cutting line, tapering in to the lower bust dart line. Make the grain line parallel to the center front.

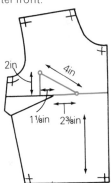

9 To mark pocket position, extend top line of bust dart to center front edge. From dart point measure in along this line 2⅜in (6cm) and mark with a circle. Returning to dart point, measure 1⅛in (3cm) toward side seam along top dart line and mark. From this mark draw a line at a right angle and measure off 2in (5cm). Mark this point with a circle. Join circles. This is the pocket line and will be about 4in (10cm) long.

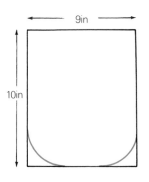

10 For pocket pattern, draw a rectangle 9 × 10in (23cm by 25.5cm). Using a flexible curve, redraw bottom corners.

John Hutchinson

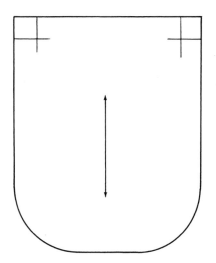

11 Mark the grain line parallel to the side edges. Mark in the seam allowance of $\frac{5}{8}$in (1.5cm) which has been included on all edges.

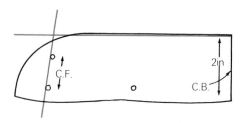

12 To make the collar pattern, trace the shirt collar band pattern, leaving extra paper around all edges. Draw a line through the center front. To make the collar wider, measure up the center back and the center front line from the neck seamline 2in (5cm). Draw a line across the top edge of the collar connecting these two points.

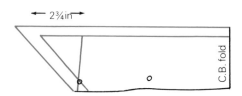

13 To make the collar point, extend a line out from the center front line 2¾in (7cm) and mark. Connect this point to the center front seamline at the neck edge. Add $\frac{5}{8}$in (1.5cm) seam allowance to top and front edge of new collar shape.

14 To make the pants front pattern, trace the basic pants front pattern, omitting the waist dart. To narrow the pants leg at the hem, mark the hemline on the tracing by drawing a line across the pattern at a right angle to the grain line. Measure in along the hemline from the inside and outside leg cutting lines 1⅜in (3.5cm) and mark.

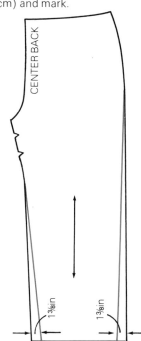

15 Using a yardstick, redraw the new inside leg cutting line from the hemline up, tapering into the original cutting line at the lower notch. Re-draw the new outside leg cutting line, tapering into the original cutting line at the hip line.

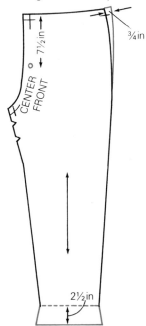

16 Add a 2½in (6.5cm) hem allowance to the lower edge, and re-shape the side edges of the hem as shown in Volume 10, page 61.

17 Measure in ¾in (2cm) along the waist cutting line from the side cutting line. Draw a line down from this point to the hip line. Mark the $\frac{5}{8}$in (1.5cm) seam allowances which have been included on side and top edges. For the zipper position, measure down the center front seamline from the waist cutting line 7½in (19cm) and mark.

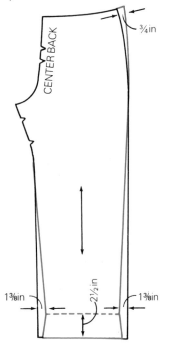

18 For the pants back pattern, trace the basic pants back omitting the waist dart. Using the same measurements as for the pants front, make the leg narrower, tapering inside and outside legs and adjusting the hem as before.
19 Measure in along the waist cutting line from the side cutting line ¾in (2cm) and draw the new side cutting line down from this point to the hip line. Cut around the new pants shape. Mark the $\frac{5}{8}$in (1.5cm) seam allowances which have been included on the side and top edges.

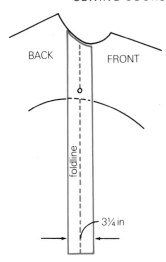

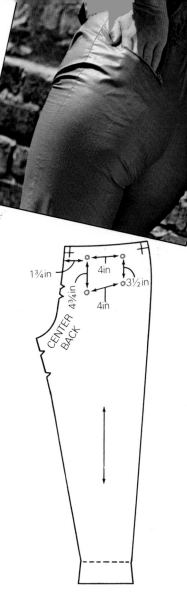

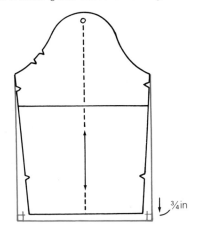

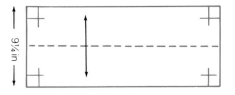

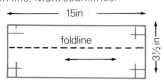

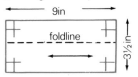

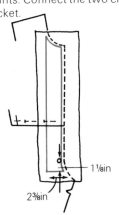

pattern pieces together on the waist seamline. Trace the neck edge and the center front edge of the bodice and pants down to the circle which marks the zipper position. Add 1⅛in (3cm) to this length and make facing 2⅜in (6cm) wide as shown in diagram.

22 Mark the grain line parallel to the center front edge and mark the ⅝in (1.5cm) seam allowances at the neck edge and the center front edge.

23 To make the sleeve pattern, trace the shirt sleeve pattern. Mark the grain line, extending it to the sleeve cap and hem edge. Mark the lengthening and shortening line.

24 Add ¾in (2cm) to the lower edge of sleeve and draw a line across the pattern. Using a right triangle, aligned with the lengthening and shortening line, straighten the side edges of the sleeve. Draw the new cutting lines, starting from the original cutting line at underarm curve to new cutting line at the lower edge.

20 To mark the pocket position on the pants back pattern, measure out along the waist seamline from the center back seamline 1¾in (4.5cm) and then a further 4in (10cm). From these two points draw two lines down from the waist seamline parallel to the grainline. This first line is 4¾in (12cm) long and the second line is 3½in (9cm) long. Mark a circle at each of these points. Connect the two circles to mark pocket.

21 To make the front facing pattern, pin the front bodice and the pants front

25 Mark ⅝in (1.5cm) seam allowances. The grain line will be the center positioning line for the contrast strap.

26 To make cuff pattern, draw a rectangle to same measurement as lower edge of sleeve measuring 9¼in (23.5cm) deep. Mark foldline across center of rectangle and grain line parallel to short edges. Mark seam allowances, which have been included in these measurements.

27 To make contrasting strap pattern, measure the full length of the sleeve, not including the seam allowances, at the sleeve cap. Draw a rectangle to this length by 3¼in (8.5cm) wide, leaving extra paper at top. A ⅝in (1.5cm) seam allowance has been included on both side edges. Draw a line up from center of strap, extending it for a few inches.

28 To add the shoulder length and to mark the neck curve at top edge of strap, pin the front and back bodice pattern pieces together along the shoulder seamline. Place the strap pattern over the bodices, matching the shoulder points and the armhole seamlines, and the center strap line with the shoulder seamline.

29 Extend strap pattern as far as neck cutting line, following neck curve. Remove strap pattern. The center line is the grain line. Mark seamlines.

30 To make right front belt pattern, draw a rectangle 3½in (9cm) wide by 15in (38cm) long. These measurements are for a size 10. For each larger size add an extra 1in (2.5cm) to length. Seam allowances are included. Mark foldline along center and grain line parallel to it.

31 To make left front belt pattern, draw a rectangle 3½in (9cm) wide by 9in (23cm) long for a size 10. For each larger size add an extra 1in (2.5cm) to length. Seam allowances have been included. Mark foldline and grain line as before.

Elasticized cuffs

Elasticized cuffs, as shown on the jump-suit on page 82, are easy to make and give a sporty look. They are useful too; if sleeves are too short, if cuffs or sleeve hems are frayed and need renewing, if wrists need to be kept warm and dry—elasticized cuffs will solve the problem. The width of the cuff piece measures the same as the end of the sleeve, plus seam allowances. The depth of the cuff piece is equal to twice the finished depth of the cuff, plus seam allowances. Mark a fold-line down the middle of the cuff, along its length.

1 With right sides facing, baste and stitch the cuff ends together, stitching from the outer edge to the foldline on one side only. Press seam open.

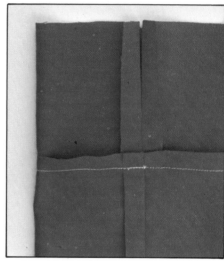

2 With right sides together and seams matching, baste and stitch the cuff to the lower edge of the sleeve. Press cuff away from sleeve, trim seam allowances and press them toward cuff.

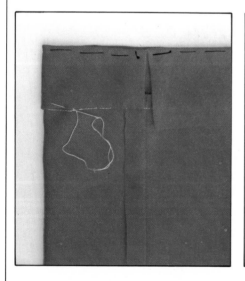

3 Fold the cuff to the inside along the foldline. Baste along folded edge. Turn under ⅝in (1.5cm) seam allowance around the free edge of the cuff and slip stitch it to the stitching line, leaving the cuff seam open on the inside for inserting the elastic.

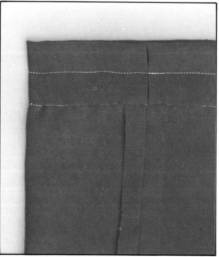

4 Run a line of machine stitching along the center of the cuff, starting and finishing the stitching at the seam to form two casings for the elastic. Repeat with the second cuff. Press.

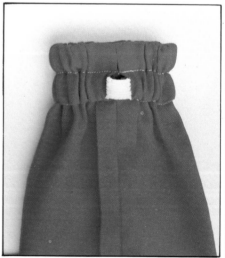

5 Cut four pieces of elastic to fit around the wrist comfortably. Insert two pieces of elastic into each cuff through the opening at the seam. Sew ends of elastic together, overlapping them slightly. Push the elastic ends into each casing and slip stitch the seam edges together to close the opening.

Simon Butcher

Attaching stretch cuffs

Simon Butcher

1 This method uses a pair of ready-made, knitted cuffs. After machine gathering the sleeve hem seamline, finish raw edge with overcasting. Slide the cuff over the sleeve with right sides together, edges even. Stretch the cuff slightly and pull up the gathering threads of sleeve to fit. Pin and baste on seamline.

2 Stitch the cuff to the sleeve over the basting, using a stretch stitch or a narrow zig-zag stitch so that the cuff can stretch. Or, stretch the cuff as you stitch; the threads will pucker slightly when released but will stretch to fit the hand when worn.

3 Remove the basting and gently press the seam toward the sleeve from the wrong side. From the right side of the garment, press the seamline only, using a pressing cloth and the point of the iron.

Jumpsuit (2)

Skate off in this stylish suit, begun on page 77.

Directions for making

Suggested fabrics
Ciré, poplin, corduroy, glazed cotton or satin.

Materials
45in (115cm)-wide fabric with or without nap:
Sizes 10, 12: 4⅜yd (4m)
Sizes 14, 16: 4⅝yd (4.2m)
Sizes 18, 20: 4¾yd (4.3m)
45in (115cm)-wide contrasting fabric without nap:
For all sizes: ½yd (.5m)

36in (90cm)-wide interfacing:
For all sizes: ¼yd (.2m)
Thread; four 4in (10cm) zippers
Heavy-duty zipper: 24in (61cm) long (for size 10); for larger sizes measure pattern omitting seam allowances
¾in (2cm)-wide elastic:
Sizes 10-14: 1¾yd (1.5m)
Sizes 16-20: 2¼yd (2m)
1 snap fastener
1⅛in (3cm)-wide buckle, with or without prong; metal belt eyelets (for buckle with prong only)

Key to adjusted pattern pieces

A	Back bodice	Cut 2
B	Front bodice	Cut 2
C	Back pleat underlay	Cut 1 (contrast)
D	Collar	Cut 2 on fold (1 in contrast)
E	Pocket	Cut 8
F	Pants front	Cut 2
G	Pants back	Cut 2
H	Front facing	Cut 2
I	Sleeve	Cut 2
J	Cuff	Cut 2
K	Sleeve and shoulder strap	Cut 2 (contrast)
L	Right front belt	Cut 1
M	Left front belt	Cut 1

Interfacing: use pieces **D**, **L** and **M**, cut to half width only.

1 Prepare the fabric and cut out the pattern pieces. Transfer all pattern markings before removing the pattern pieces. Make the front bust darts and press downward.

2 Make the pockets on the bodice front sections and pants back sections as shown on page 74.

45in-wide fabric without nap (contrast)

single fabric

K

K

D

C

selvage

selvage

Interfacing: 36in-wide fabric

D

L+M

selvages

fold

45in-wide fabric with or without nap

fold

open out fabric to cut

cut 1

cut 1

G

J J

M

B

L

D

E

F

A

I

H   E E E

selvages

Brian Mayor

Stuart Macleod

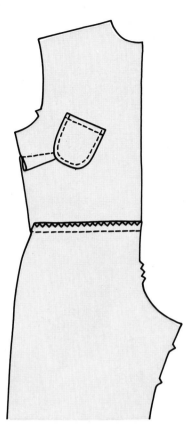

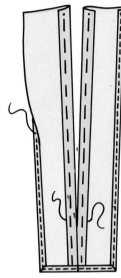

marked circle to within 2in (5cm) of the inside leg seam. Clip curve and press seam open. Fold in $\frac{5}{8}$in (1.5cm) seam allowance along both center front edges of the bodice and pants. Baste and press flat.

tape. Adjust the facing so that the teeth do not catch when the zipper is opened or closed.

3 With right sides together, baste and stitch the bodice fronts to the pants fronts taking a $\frac{5}{8}$in (1.5cm) seam. Finish the seam allowances. Press the seam upward.

5 Pin and baste the zipper inside of center front opening, bringing the center fronts together. With right sides together, baste and stitch the short center front seam of the front facing to the lower edge. Press seam open. Turn in the seam allowance along the center front edges of the facing and baste. Press flat. To finish the outer edge of the facing, turn in $\frac{1}{4}$in (6mm) and machine stitch.

7 Using the zipper foot and working from the right side of the garment, stitch along both sides and across the bottom of the zipper, stitching through all thicknesses. Remove basting and press. Check that facing is stitched through on wrong side; if not, slip stitch to zipper tape.

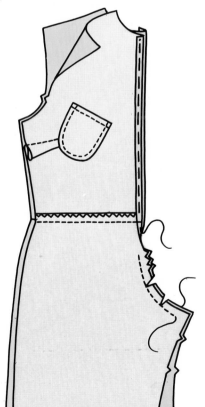

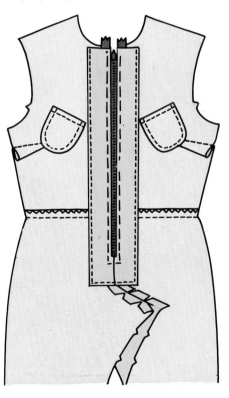

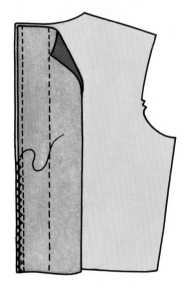

4 With right sides together, baste and stitch the front crotch seam from the

6 With the wrong sides of the facing to the wrong side of the garment, pin and baste the facing down over the zipper

8 Mark the center back pleat foldline on the bodice backs and the center back line on the pleat underlay piece. With right sides together, baste and stitch the pleat underlay to the bodice backs. Finish all the seam allowances and press flat.

Terry Evans

83

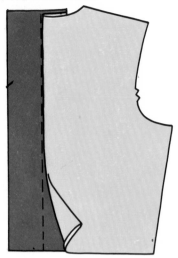

9 Fold the bodice along the pleat foldline, wrong sides together, bringing the pleat to the center back line of the underlay. Press the folded edge. Join other bodice back to pleat underlay.

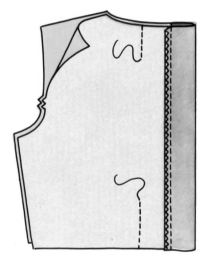

10 Keeping the two center back (fold) lines together and working from the wrong side, baste and stitch the two bodice pieces together along the folds from the neck edge down to the first circle and from the lower edge up to the second circle.

11 Fold the bodice pieces back to form the pleat on the right side. Baste across

the neck and waistline edges of the pleat to hold it in place.

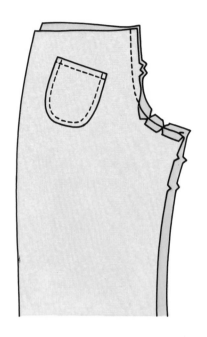

12 With right sides together, baste and stitch the center back crotch seam from top edge to within 2in (5cm) of inside leg seam. Clip curve and press seam open.

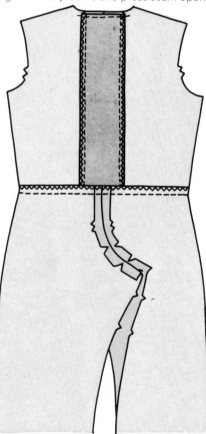

13 With right sides together and center backs matching, baste and stitch the bodice back to the pants back. Finish

seam allowances and press upward. Remove basting.

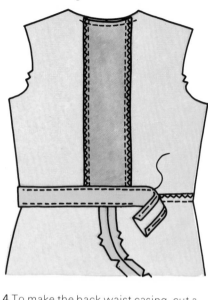

14 To make the back waist casing, cut a piece of fabric 2in (5cm) wide and the same measurement as the back waist seam including allowances. Turn in $\frac{1}{2}$in (1.2cm) on both long edges and baste. Press flat. With wrong sides together, center the casing over the back waist seamline and baste it in place. Stitch the casing close to each long edge. Press.

15 Cut a piece of elastic to fit across back waist comfortably. Insert the elastic through the casing and anchor it at the side seams with a row of stitching.

16 With right sides together, baste and stitch the shoulder seams, pressing them open. Mark the strap position on the center of the sleeve with basting. Run two rows of gathering stitches around the sleeve cap between notches. With right sides together, matching shoulder points and notches, pin the sleeve into the armhole, pulling up the gathering threads to ease the fullness. Baste and stitch, spreading the fullness evenly over the sleeve cap.

17 Press the seam allowance together, trimming them to $\frac{3}{8}$in (1cm) wide. Finish the seam allowances and press toward the sleeve.

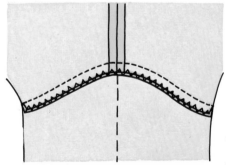

18 Prepare the strap and stitch it to the sleeve and bodice as explained for the strap seam on page 75.

Terry Evans

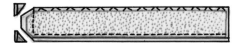

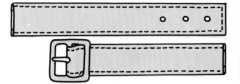

19 Baste the interfacing to the wrong side of each belt piece and catch-stitch it to the foldline. Fold each belt section right sides together along the foldline. Baste and stitch across one short end and along the edge opposite the fold. Trim the interfacing close to the stitching. Clip corners. Press.

20 Turn the belts right side out. Baste around the edges. Press. Topstitch all around, $\frac{1}{4}$in (6mm) in from edge. Press. For a slide belt, stitch buckle to left-hand belt. If using a buckle with prong, make 3 or 4 eyelets on right-hand belt, using an eyelet kit. Also make one eyelet on the left-hand belt so that the buckle prong can be inserted through it. Attach the buckle to the stitched end of the left-hand belt and slip stitch in place.

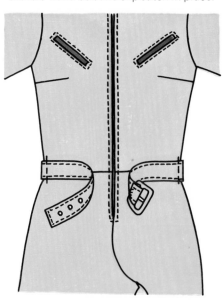

21 Baste the belt sections to each side of the front pieces over the waist seamline. With right sides together, matching armhole seams and waistline seams, baste and stitch the side seams from the lower edges of the pants to the lower edge of the sleeves. Finish and press seams open.

22 With right sides together, baste and stitch the inside leg seams. Finish and press seams open. With right sides together and inside leg seams matching, complete the stitching around crotch seam. Press seam open. Try on the jumpsuit, turn up the pants hems and blind-hem.

Stuart Macleod

23 Baste the interfacing to the wrong side of the top collar section. With right sides together and edges even, baste and stitch both collar sections together, leaving the neck edge open. Trim the interfacing close to the stitching. Trim seam allowance and clip corners. Turn the collar right side out. Baste around the outer edge of the collar. Press.

24 With right sides together, matching center backs, shoulder points and center fronts, baste the interfaced edge of collar

to neck edge. Stitch around entire neck edge. Trim the interfacing close to stitching. Grade seam allowances and clip curves. Press seam allowances toward collar.

Terry Evans

25 On the inside of the neck edge, turn under the seam allowance of the under-collar and slip stitch to the neck seamline. Press. On the right side, topstitch $\frac{1}{4}$in (6mm) in from edge of collar, ending stitching at center front edge. Press. Sew a snap fastener to the collar extension as shown.

26 Complete cuff and attach to sleeve. Insert elastic as directed on page 80.

Needlework / COURSE 15

* Contemporary pulled thread work
* Designing a pulled thread lampshade cover
* More pulled thread stitches
* A lampshade cover to make

Contemporary pulled thread work

Pulled thread work is perhaps most often used for delicate, symmetrical designs such as the sachet and stocking bag featured in Needlework course 12, Volume 9, page 78. But it can be used equally well to create bold, free-flowing designs—as the lampshade cover on page 87 demonstrates. The stitches are used here to create areas of contrasting texture within a pattern of seemingly random flowing lines. The movement of the linear design is enhanced by the spontaneous way of working the satin stitch lines and the eyelets.

This style of work is well-suited to coarse, loosely-woven fabrics, such as burlap and various curtain fabrics. You can use it to create imaginative accessories for yourself and your home—lacy shawls, curtains, screens and dramatic wall hangings. If you like the textures of pulled thread work but find counting threads meticulously a bit tedious, you'll enjoy working in this relaxed style.

Designing a pulled thread lampshade cover

Many different kinds of design could be effectively used for a lampshade cover. If your shade is cylindrical, you might like to echo its shape with rectangular blocks and bands of stitches, perhaps intersecting one another. A plaid fabric or one of Mondrian's paintings could serve as inspiration.

If your shade is conical, the fabric will cover it on the bias, and any horizontal elements in the design will curve downward, while vertical elements will lie at varying angles. This can be effective, but as a general rule it is better to use curving lines, which exploit the diagonals of the shade and the mounted fabric.

If you have a flair for drawing, you can design directly on the lampshade pattern (first drawn as described in step 1, page 88). Otherwise, you can find suitable designs in the natural world. The grain of a piece of wood, the ripples in a pond or the outline of a river on a map are some of the many possible sources. Photographic magazines often include photos of natural objects emphasizing their patterns. If design material doesn't make itself obvious, you can use the "finder" technique (see Volume 8, page 87). Alternatively, you could take your own photographs—a very good way to develop an eye for good design. For pulled thread work, black and white photographs are preferable, as you can concentrate on line and texture without the distraction of color.

When you have found several possible patterns, make a tracing of each. Enlarge them to fit the lampshade pattern (see Volume 4, page 76).

In deciding which stitches to use, remember that in pulled thread work design is expressed mainly in contrasting textures, rather than lines. Notice how the designer of our lampshade cover has achieved this. The outer area is worked in a small, regular pattern (wave stitch); next comes an area of strong, irregular verticals (satin stitch) and then a richly textured area of free eyelets, bounded on the right by a small area of wave stitch. The eyelets—the most interesting element —are repeated, less densely, at the upper curve of the design. Repetition is an important element in many kinds of design (think of musical phrases, for example). Often the repetition is more effective if it is varied slightly. Here, the scattered eyelets are used as a kind of visual "echo." Similarly, the lines of three-sided stitch outside the main area repeat and emphasize its shape without following it exactly.

 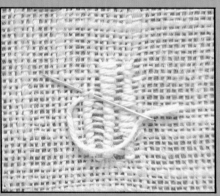 

Wave stitch is basically zig-zag back stitch (see Volume 9, page 78) but is here worked to fill an area. Work from top to bottom, over 2, 3, or 4 threads, depending on the size of the area and the scale desired.

Satin stitch may be worked over varying numbers of threads to produce lines of different thickness. The variations in width within the line are produced by altering the tension. Some threads can be left unworked to provide further variety.

Free eyelets are simply eyelets (see Volume 9, page 78) worked over an irregular number of threads, generally with the hole off-center. Some are left partially unworked. If the hole becomes too congested with threads—which can happen as you work around a corner—work into alternate spaces rather than into every one.

Three-sided stitch Bring needle up at point A. Make two backstitches between B and A. Make a backstitch between C and A, then take needle down at C and up at D. Make two backstitches between C and D. Make a backstitch between A and D, then take the needle down at A and bring it up at E. Continue in the same pattern, pulling stitches tightly as shown at far right. The stitch can also be worked along the straight grain.

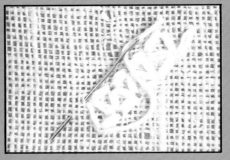

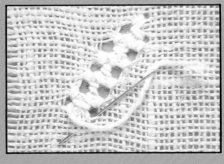

Light lines

Flowing lines and a fascinating interplay of textures make an elegant pulled thread cover for a modern lampshade. Use our design or make one of your own.

Materials

Plain conical or cylindrical lampshade
Sheet of paper large enough to wrap around lampshade and not too stiff
One or more large sheets of tracing paper
Coarse evenweave fabric, burlap or similar furnishing fabric (amount determined as in step 5 below); the linen fabric used for the lampshade has 13 threads to 1in (2.5cm)
Thread of similar weight to those in fabric and matching in color; you can use threads unraveled from fabric
Tapestry needle
Embroidery hoop
Ruler
Paper clips
Fabric glue
Woven tape or braid

Embroidering the shade cover

1 Begin by making a paper pattern of your lampshade. Wrap the paper smoothly around the shade, turning it under at top and bottom edges and securing it with paper clips as shown. Mark the side seam of the shade on the paper. Remove the paper from the shade and cut along the folds and the marked side seamlines.

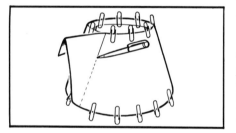

2 Place a yardstick or other long straight-edge on the pattern, aligning it with the two outer points, and draw in a grain line, as on the design shown opposite.
3 Lay the pattern on a flat surface and place a sheet of tracing paper over it. Draw the pattern outline, then draw curved lines over the pattern. You can use our design as a guide or make your own (see page 86). At this stage you needn't decide on the stitches to be used, but you should draw in the areas to be filled with different stitches, as in the design shown here.
4 Cut out the design area and place it on the lampshade to see how it works in the round. Repeat step 3 if necessary until you get a pleasing design.
5 Measure the lampshade pattern and buy enough fabric to leave a margin of at least 3in (7.5cm) all around, plus a little extra (big enough to fit your embroidery hoop) for practice. Also buy the embroidery thread.
6 Using the extra fabric, work samples of your chosen stitches. You can use the ones shown here or in Needlework course 12, Volume 9, page 78, or other stitches shown in books on pulled thread work. Hold the samples against the shade, with the lamp turned on, to see if they are the correct scale for the shade. Shapes tend to be reduced in silhouette.
7 Pin the original lampshade pattern to the fabric, aligning the grain line with the lengthwise grain of the fabric. Baste around the edge, but **do not cut out the fabric**; for the shape may become distorted while you are working the embroidery.
8 Pin each paper shape, in turn, to the fabric and baste around it. Lines, such as the line of three-sided stitch used for our

design, can be indicated with a single line of basting. Or you can work them "freehand" when the rest of the embroidery is completed. The designer of the shade cover shown also added a few scattered free eyelets at the inner curve.
9 Now work the embroidery, completing one area of stitching before going on to the next.

Assembling the shade cover

1 Press the embroidery well on the wrong side, first placing it over a thick folded towel or blanket covered with a sheet.
2 Pin the two side edges together, with wrong sides facing, along the marked lines; baste.
3 Pull the cover over the shade. Often the embroidery draws in the fabric; if this has happened, mark in the new top and bottom edges with basting and remove the original stitches. Remove cover from shade. Trim side seam allowances to 1in (2.5cm).
4 Remove basting joining side seam. Stitch three rows of overlapping zig-zag ¾in (2cm) outside the marked top and bottom edges to prevent fraying. Trim away fabric outside zig-zag stitches.
5 Baste and stitch the side seam with right sides facing. Add a few rows of zig-zag just outside the seam, working through both layers. Trim seam.
6 Pull the completed cover over the shade, aligning the seam with that of the shade. Apply a line of fabric glue to the bottom inner rim of the shade and to the corresponding edges of the fabric. Glue fabric in place, pressing firmly. Repeat on top edge, pulling the fabric to tension it as you work. Allow glue to dry thoroughly.
7 Cover the raw edges of the fabric with the tape or braid, gluing it in place.

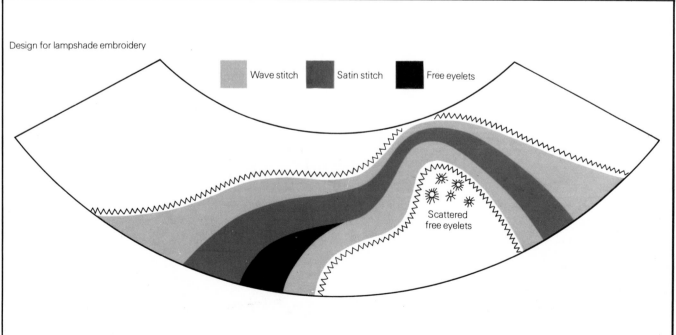

Design for lampshade embroidery

Wave stitch Satin stitch Free eyelets

Scattered free eyelets

John Hutchinson

EXTRA SPECIAL CROCHET

Subtle choice of colors make these turtlenecks suitable for "boys" of any age. The harmonizing tones of the diamond shapes are brought into sharper relief by the contrasting stitch textures.

Like father, like son

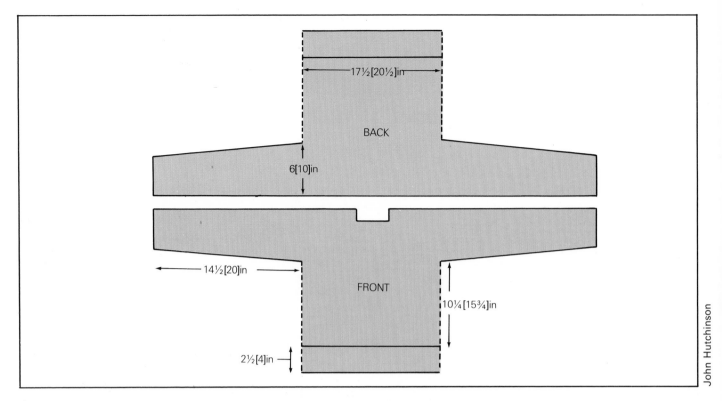

On the diagram:
17½[20½]in
BACK
6[10]in
14½[20]in
FRONT
10¼[15¾]in
2½[4]in

John Hutchinson

Sizes
To fit 26/28[38/40]in (66/71[97/102] cm) chest.
Length, 18[27½]in (46[70]cm).
Sleeve seam, 14½[20]in (37[51]cm).
Note: Directions for larger size are in brackets [ ]; if there is only one set of figures, it applies to both sizes.

Materials
Knitting worsted
19[36]oz (475[900]g) in color A
4oz (100g) in color B
4[6]oz (100[150]g) in color C
3[4]oz (75[100]g) in color D
2[3]oz (50[75]g) in color E
Size F (4.00mm) crochet hook

Gauge
20 sts and 24 rows to 4in (10cm) in seed st worked with size F (4.00mm) hook.

Single crochet diamonds
Using size F (4.00mm) hook and D, make 2ch, work 1sc into 2nd ch from hook. Turn.
1st row 1ch, 2sc into the 1sc. Turn.
2nd row 1ch, 2sc into each of the 2sc. Turn.
3rd row 1ch, 1sc into each of the 4sc. Turn.
4th row 1ch, 2sc into first sc, 1sc into each of next 2sc, 2sc into last sc. Turn. 6sc.
5th row 1ch, 1sc into each sc to end. Turn.
6th row 1ch, 2sc into first sc, 1sc into each sc to within last sc, 2sc into last sc. Turn. 8sc.
7th row As 5th.
Cont in this way, inc one st at each end of every alternate row until diamond measures 4[5½]in (10[14]cm) across; end with straight row.

Next row 1ch, leaving loop of each on hook, work 1sc into each of next 2sc, yo and draw a loop through all loops on hook—1sc dec—, 1sc into each sc to within last 2sc, dec 1sc. Turn.
Next row 1ch, 1sc into each sc to end. Turn.
Rep last 2 rows until 2 sts rem. Work 2 tog. Fasten off. Make 7 more diamonds.

Bobble diamonds
Using size F (4.00mm) hook and C make 2ch, 1sc into 2nd ch from hook. Turn.
1st row 1ch, 3sc into the 1sc. Turn.
2nd row 1ch, sl st into first sc, yo, insert hook into next st, yo and draw loop through, yo and draw loop through first loop on hook, yo, insert hook into same st, yo and draw loop through, yo and draw loop through 4 loops on hook, yo and draw through rem 2 loops—bobble made or MB—, sl st into last sc. Turn.
3rd row 1ch, 2sc into first sl st, 1sc into bobble, 2sc into last sl st. Turn.
4th row 1ch, sl st into first sc, MB into next sc, sl st into next sc, MB into next sc, sl st into last sc. Turn.
5th row 1ch, 2sc into first sl st, (1sc into next bobble, 1sc into next sl st) to within last sl st, 2sc into last sl st. Turn.
6th row 1ch, sl st into first sc, (MB into next sc, sl st into next sc) to within last sc, sl st into last sc. Turn.
Rep last 2 rows until diamond measures 4[5½]in (10[14]cm) across; end with bobble row.
Next row 1ch, dec 1sc, 1sc into each st to within last 2 sts, dec 1sc. Turn.
Next row 1ch, sl st into first sc, (MB into next sc, sl st into next sc) to within last sc, sl st into last sc. Turn.

Rep last 2 rows until 3 sts rem. Work 1 row bobbles, then work the 3 sts tog. Fasten off. Make 7 more diamonds.

Half double diamonds
Using size F (4.00mm) hook and B make 3ch, work 1hdc into 3rd ch from hook. Turn.
1st row 2ch, 1hdc into first hdc, 2hdc into top of turning ch. Turn.
2nd row 2ch, 1hdc into first hdc, 1hdc into each st to end, 1hdc into top of ch. Turn.
3rd row As 2nd.
4th row 2ch, 1hdc into first hdc, 1hdc into each st to end, 2hdc into top of ch. Turn.
Rep last 3 rows until work measures 4[5½]in (10[14]cm) across.
1st dec row 2ch, skip first hdc, leaving last loop of each on hook work 1hdc into each of next 2 sts, yo and draw through all loops on hook—1hdc dec—, 1hdc into each st to end. Turn.
2nd dec row As 1st dec row.
3rd dec row 2ch, skip first hdc, dec 1 hdc, work to within last 3 sts, dec 1hdc, 1hdc into top of 2ch. Turn. Rep last 3 rows until 3 sts rem, work 3 tog. Fasten off. Make 7 more diamonds.

Half diamond
Using size F (4.00mm) hook and A, make 3ch.
1st row 1sc into 2nd ch from hook, 1sc into next ch. Turn.
2nd row 2ch, sl st into first sc, 1hdc into next sc, sl st into same sc. Turn. 4 sts.
3rd row 2ch, skip first sl st, sl st into next hdc, 1hdc into next sl st, sl st into top of 2ch. Turn.
4th row 1ch, sl st into first sl st, 1hdc into

same sl st, sl st into next hdc, 1 hdc into next sl st, sl st and 1 hdc into top of 2ch. Turn.
5th row 1ch, sl st into first hdc, 1 hdc into next sl st, sl st into next hdc, 1 hdc into next sl st. Turn.
6th row 2ch, sl st into first hdc, (1 hdc into next sl st, sl st into next hdc) to last sl st, 1 hdc and sl st into last sl st. Turn.
7th row 2ch, skip first sl st, (sl st into next hdc, 1 hdc, into next sl st) to last 2ch, sl st into top of 2ch. Turn.
8th row 1ch, sl st into first sl st, 1 hdc into same sl st, (sl st into next hdc, 1 hdc into next sl st) to last 2ch, sl st and 1 hdc into top of 2ch. Turn.
9th row 1ch, sl st into first hdc, (1 hdc into next sl st, sl st into next hdc) to last sl st, 1 hdc into last sl st. Turn. Rep rows 6 to 9 inclusive until there are 19[25] sts and work measures 4[5½]in (10[14]cm) across. Fasten off. Make 7 more half diamonds in A, then work 8 half diamonds in E.

Sleeves and yoke sections
Back
Using size F (4.00mm) hook and A, make 6ch, then starting at center of one half diamond in A work 1 hdc into each sl st and sl st into each hdc to end of diamond, then work across 3 more half diamonds in A, now work to center of one more half diamond, 6ch. Fasten off.
Next row Make 6ch, then working in patt, work into the first 6ch of last row, work across top of diamonds, then work into the last 6ch of last row, 6ch. Fasten off.
Rep last row 11[15] times more. 224[296] sts. Cont in patt until work measures 6[10]in (15[25]cm) from top of half diamonds.
Shape shoulders
Next row Fasten off. Skip the first 28[32] sts, rejoin yarn to next st and patt to within last 28[32] sts, turn.
Rep last row 3 times more. 32[38] sts rem for back neck. Fasten off.

Front
Rejoin A to other half of diamond at underarm and work as for back to within 10[12] rows of completion of sleeve.
Shape neck
Work across first 112[128] sts, turn. Work 9[11] rows on these sts.
Shape shoulder
Next row Fasten off. Skip first 28[32] sts, rejoin yarn to next st, work to end. Turn.
Next row Work to within last 28[32]sts, turn.
Next row Fasten off. Skip first 28[32] sts, work to end. Fasten off.
Skip center 32[38] sts for center front neck, rejoin yarn to next st and work to end. Turn.
Now work straight until sleeve measures same as first sleeve, ending at neck edge.
Shape shoulder
Next row Work to within last 28[32] sts, turn.
Next row Fasten off. Skip first 28[32] sts, work to end. Turn.

Next row Work to within last 28[32] sts. Fasten off.

Waistband
Using size F (4.00mm) hook and A, make 17[21]ch.
Base row 1 sc into 2nd ch from hook, 1 sc into each ch to end. Turn.
Patt row 1ch, working into the *back* loop only of each st, work 1 sc into each st to end. Turn. Rep last row until waistband measures 26[30]in (66[76]cm), without stretching. Fasten off.

Cuffs (make 2)
Using size F (4.00mm) hook and A, make 15[17]ch and work base row as for waistband, then work patt row until cuff measures 6[8]in (15[20]cm). Fasten off.

Collar
Using size F (4.00mm) hook and A, make 31[41]ch and work base row as for waistband, then work patt row for 15[20]in (38[51]cm). Fasten off.

To finish
Sew all diamonds tog, as shown in chart. Join upper sleeve and shoulder seams, then join underarm seams. Join short edges of collar. Join collar to neck on outside. Turn collar back. Join short edges of cuffs, then sew cuffs to sleeves. Join short edges of waistband and sew to lower edge. Press lightly if appropriate for yarn used.

CROCHET

For the well-dressed baby —a striped sweater and matching pants that make a special suit.

Suitable for baby

Sizes

Sweater To fit 18[20:22]in (46[51:56]cm) chest.
Length, 10¾[12¼:13]in (28[30:33]cm).
Sleeve seam, 5[6:6½]in (12.5[15:16.5]cm)
Pants Waist to crotch, 7[8:9]in (18[20:23]cm).
Inside leg seam, 8[9½:11½]in (20[24:29]cm).

Note Directions for larger sizes are in brackets []; if there is only one set of figures it applies to all sizes.

Materials

7[8:9]oz (180[200:220]g) of a knitting worsted in main color (A)
3[3:4]oz (60[60:80]g) in contrasting color (B)
Sizes E and G (3.50 and 4.50mm) crochet hooks
Waist length of ¾in (2cm)-wide elastic

Gauge

18 sc and 21 rows to 4in (10cm) worked on size G (4.50mm) hook.

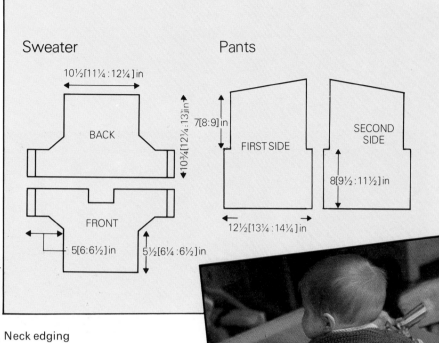

Sweater

10½[11¼:12¼]in

BACK

10¾[12¼:13]in

FRONT

5[6:6½]in

5½[6¼:6½]in

Pants

7[8:9]in

FIRST SIDE

SECOND SIDE

8[9½:11½]in

12½[13¼:14¼]in

Brian Mayor

Sweater

Back

Using size G (4.50mm) hook and B, make 47[51:55]ch.
Base row 1sc into 2nd ch from hook, 1sc into each ch to end. Turn.
Next row 1ch, 1sc into each sc to end. Turn.
Rep last row until work measures 2in (5cm) from beg. Change to A, with A work 4 rows. Change to B, with B work 4 rows. Cut off B, Cont with A until work measures 5½[6¼:6½]in (14[16:16.5]cm).
Shape sleeves
Inc row 1ch, 1sc into first sc, 2sc into next sc, 1sc into each sc to within last 2sc, 2sc into next sc, 1sc into last sc. Turn.
Rep last row 9[10:11] times more.
Next row Fasten off. Make 9[12:14] ch, then work 1sc into each sc across back, make 10[13:15] ch, turn.
Next row 1sc into 2nd ch from hook, 1sc into each ch, then 1sc into each sc across back and 1sc into each ch to end. Turn. 84[96:106]sc.
Work 16[18:20] rows without shaping. Fasten off.

Front

Work as given for back until 7[8:9] rows have been completed on sleeves.
Shape neck
Next row Work across first 31[36:41] sts, turn.
Cont on these sts until front measures same as back. Fasten off.
Skip center 22[24:26] sts for front neck, rejoin yarn to next st and work to end of row. Complete to match first side.

Neck edging

Join shoulder and upper sleeve seams. Using size E (3.50mm) hook join A to center back neck and work 1sc into each st across back neck, 1sc into each row end down neck, 1sc into each sc along front neck, 1sc into each row end up side neck, then 1 sc into each sc along back neck to center, turn.
Next row 1ch, 1sc into each sc all around Turn.
Change to B, with B rep last row 4 times. Fasten off. Join seams.

Cuffs (alike)

Using size E (3.50mm) hook join A to lower edge of sleeve and work 1sc into each row end along this edge. Turn.
Next row 1ch, 1sc into each sc to end. Turn.
Change to B. Cont in sc, work 2 rows B, 2 rows A and 6 rows B.
Fasten off. Join side and underarm seams.

Pants

First side

Using size G (4.50mm) hook and A, make 47[51:55]ch for waist edge.
Base row 1sc into 2nd ch from hook, 1sc into each ch to end. Turn.
Work 5 rows sc.
Shape back
Next row Sl st across first 4 sts, 1ch 1sc into each st to end.
Turn. 42[46:50] sts.
Next row Work to within last 4 sts, turn. 38[42:46] sts.
Rep last 2 rows twice more, then the first of these 2 rows again.
Next row Work to end across all sts. Turn. 46[50:54] sts.
** Cont straight until work measures 7[8:9]in (18[20:23]cm), measured at side edge (shortest).

Shape crotch

Next row Fasten off. Make 5ch, work 1 sc into each sc across work, 6ch, turn.
Next row 1sc into 2nd ch from hook, 1sc into each of next 4ch, 1sc into each sc to end, 1sc into each of next 5ch. Turn. 56[60:64] sc.
Cont in sc until leg measures 4[5½:7½]in (10[14:19]cm). Now work 4 rows B, 4 rows A and 12 rows B. Fasten off. **

Second side

Work as for first side to back shaping.
Next row Work to within last 4 sts, turn.
Next row Sl st across first 4 sts, 1ch, work to end. Turn.
Rep last 2 rows twice more.
Next row Work to end across all sts.
Now work as for first side from ** to **.

To finish

Join waist to crotch seam, then join inside leg seams. Work herringbone casing over elastic on WS of waist.

CROCHET

The return of the suit

A fashion classic never goes out of style and this Chanel-style suit is no exception.

Rod Delroy

Sizes
Jacket To fit 34[36:38]in (87[92:97]cm) bust.
Length, 23[23:24½]in (59[59:62]cm).
Sleeve seam, 16½[17¼:18]in (42[44:46]cm).
Skirt To fit 36[38:40]in (92[97:102]cm) hips.
Length, 26[26:27½]in (66[66:70]cm).
Note: Directions for larger sizes are in brackets []; if there is only one set of figures it applies to all sizes.

Materials
34[36:36]oz (950[1000:1000]g) of a knitting worsted in main color (A)
6oz (150g) in contrasting color (B)
Size H (5.00mm) Tunisian crochet hook
Size I (6.00mm) crochet hook
Frog fastening
A waist length of elastic +1in (2.5cm)

Gauge
18 sts and 34 rows (17 vertical loops) to 4in (10cm) worked on size H (5.00mm) Tunisian hook.

Jacket

Back
Using size H (5.00mm) Tunisian hook and A, make 80[85:90]ch. Work in plain Tunisian st until work measures 16[16:17]in (41[41:43]cm); end with a return row.
Shape armholes
Bind off 4 loops at each end of next row, then dec one loop at each end of next 6 loop rows. Cont straight until armhole measures 7[7:7½]in (18[18:19]cm); end with a return row.
Shape shoulders
Bind off 7 loops at each end of next 2 loop rows and 7[8:9] loops at each end of following loop row. Fasten off.

Left front
Using size H (5.00mm) Tunisian hook and A, make 40[43:45] ch. Work in plain Tunisian st until work measures 16[16:17]in (41[41:43]cm); end with a return row.
Shape armhole
Bind off 4 loops at beg of next row, then dec one loop at armhole edge on every loop row until 30[33:35] loops rem. Cont straight until armhole measures 6[6:6¼]in (15[15:16]cm); end with a return row.

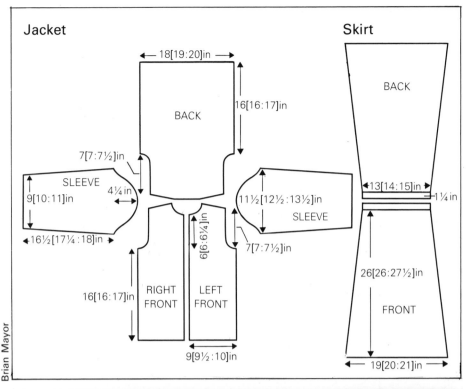

Jacket

BACK — 18[19:20]in, 16[16:17]in

SLEEVE — 7[7:7½]in, 4¼ in, 9[10:11]in, 16½[17¼:18]in

RIGHT FRONT, LEFT FRONT — 16[16:17]in, 6[6:6¼]in, 9[9½:10]in

SLEEVE — 11½[12½:13½]in, 7[7:7½]in

Skirt

BACK — 13[14:15]in, 1¼ in, 26[26:27½]in

FRONT — 19[20:21]in

Brian Mayor

Join A to lower edge of sleeve and work 2 rows sc. Fasten off.

Pocket flaps (make 2)
Using size H (5.00mm) Tunisian hook and A, make 20ch. Work 16 rows plain Tunisian st (8 vertical loops).
Next row Work 1 sc into each vertical loop to end, Fasten off.

To finish
Join shoulder seams. Set in sleeves, then join side and sleeve seams.

Trim
Using size I (6.00mm) crochet hook and B, make 4ch.
Next row Insert hook into 2nd ch from hook, yo and draw a loop through, (insert hook into next ch, yo and draw a loop through) twice. 4 loops.
Next row Yo and draw a loop through first loop on hook, (yo and draw through next 2 loops on hook) to end.
Next 2 rows Insert hook from right to left under 3rd vertical loop, yo and draw a loop through, insert hook from right to left under 2nd vertical loop so twisting 2 loops, yo and draw a loop through, insert hook into last loop, yo and draw a loop through, then work back. Rep last 2 rows until trim fits all around edge of jacket. Fasten off.
Work trim to fit around armholes and along shoulder seams, around cuffs and around 3 sides of pocket flaps.
Sew on trim and frog fastening.

Skirt

Back
Using size H (5.00mm) Tunisian hook and A, make 86[91:96] ch. Work in plain Tunisian st until work measures 19½[19½: 20½]in (50[50:52]cm); end with a return row.
1st dec row Dec 1 loop, work 25[27:29] loops, dec one loop, work 26[27:28] loops, dec one loop, work 25[27:29] loops, dec one loop, work 1 loop. Work 7 rows straight (3 vertical loops).
2nd dec row Dec 1 loop, work 24[26:28] loops, dec one loop, work 24[25:26] loops, dec one loop, work 24[26:28] loops, dec one loop, work 1 loop. Cont to dec in this way, working 1 loop less between each dec at sides and 2 loops less at center panel until 58[64:68] loops rem. Cont straight until work measures 26[26:27½]in (66[66:70]cm). Work 6 rows sc. Fasten off. Work 2 rows sc along lower edge.

Front
Work as for back.

To finish
Join side seams. Work herringbone casing over elastic on WS at waist.

Shape neck
Next 2 rows Work to within last 5[7:8] loops, then work back. Dec one loop at neck edge on every loop row until 21[24:27] loops rem. Cont straight until armhole measures 7[7:7½]in (18[18: 19]cm); end at armhole edge.

Shape shoulder
Bind off 7 loops at beg of next 2 loop rows.
Next row Work to end. Fasten off.

Right front
As left front, reversing all shaping.

Sleeves
Using size H (5.00mm) Tunisian hook and A, make 42[46:50] ch.
Work in plain Tunisian st, inc one loop at each end of every foll 12th loop row until there are 52[56:60] loops. Cont straight until work measures 16½[17¼: 18]in (42[44:46]cm).

Shape top
Bind off 4 loops at each end of next row, then dec one st at each end of 6 alternate rows, then at each end of next 6 loop rows.
Fasten off.

Disco beat

These dazzling disco socks will put you in the top ten.

Maroon socks

Sizes
Foot length, 9½in (24cm).
Leg including heel, 22in (56cm).

Materials
8oz (200g) of a sport yarn
Contrasting yarn for embroidery
1 pair of No. 2 (2¾mm) knitting needles; large tapestry needle

Gauge
28 sts and 36 rows to 4in (10cm) in stockinette stitch on No. 2 (2¾mm) needles.

To make
Cast on 73 sts.
1st ribbing row K1, (P1, K1) to end.
2nd ribbing row P1, (K1, P1) to end.
Rep these 2 rows for 1in (2.5cm); end with a 2nd ribbing row.
Beg with a K row, cont in stockinette st until work measures 13½in (34.5cm); end with a P row.

Shape leg
Dec one st at each end of next and every foll 8th row until 65 sts rem. Cont without shaping until work measures 20in (51cm); end with a P row. Cut off yarn.

Divide for instep
Next row Sl first 16 sts onto a length of

yarn, rejoin yarn to next st and K across center 33 sts, sl last 16 sts onto a length of yarn. Work in stockinette st on center 33 sts for 5½in (14cm) for instep; end with a P row.

Shape toe
Dec one st at each end of next and every

foll alternate row until 13 sts rem. P1 row. Bind off.
Join back seam.
Place the 2 sets of 16 sts on one needle. With RS facing join on yarn and work on these 32 sts for heel as foll:
1st row K15, sl 1, K1, psso, K to end. 31 sts.
2nd row P.
3rd row *Sl 1, K1, rep from * to last 3 sts, sl 1, K2.
Rep last 2 rows 13 times more, then work the 2nd row again.
Turn heel
1st row K19, K2 tog, turn.
2nd row P8, P2 tog, turn.
3rd row K8, K2 tog, turn.
Rep last 2 rows until all sts have been worked, ending with a 2nd row. 9 sts.
Next row (RS) K9, pick up 16 sts along side of heel.
Next row P25, pick up 16 sts along other side of heel. 41 sts.
Cont in stockinette st, dec one st at each end of next and every foll alternate row until 33 sts rem. Cont without shaping until work measures same as instep to beg of toe shaping.
Shape toe
Dec one st at each end of next and every

foll alternate row until 13 sts rem. P1 row. Bind off.

To finish
Join foot seams. Embroider motifs around top of sock if you like; we have chosen matchstick men.

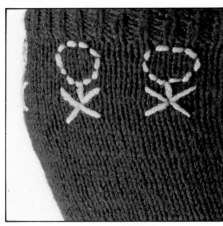

Lacy socks with ruffle

Sizes Foot length, 9½in (24cm).
Leg including heel, 7in (18cm).

Materials
4oz (100g) of a lightweight cotton yarn in a plain color (A)
2oz (50g) in a contrasting color (B)
1 set of four No. 1 (2½mm) knitting needles
Size B (2.50mm) crochet hook

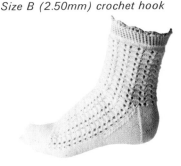

To make
Using three of No. 1 (2½mm) needles and A, cast on 30 sts onto first needle and 24 sts onto each of 2nd and 3rd needles. Using 4th needle, beg patt.
1st round *P2, K3, P1, rep from * to end.
2nd round *P2, yo, sl 1, K2 tog, psso, yo, P1, rep from * to end.
3rd and 4th rounds K to end.
These 4 rounds form patt. Rep them until work measures 4in (10cm) from beg.
Shape heel
Next row K18, then sl last 18 sts of round onto other end of same needle.
These 36 sts are for heel. Divide rem 42 sts onto 2 needle and leave for instep.
Beg with a P row, work 27 rows stockinette st on heel sts.
Next row K22, K2 tog, turn.
Next row P9, P2 tog, turn.

Next row K10, K2 tog, turn.
Cont in this way until all sts are worked on one row again. 22 sts. K11 sts to complete heel.
Work instep
Sl all instep sts onto 1 needle again; using first needle, K rem 11 heel sts, pick up and K 17 sts from side of heel; using 2nd needle patt across instep sts; using 3rd needle, pick up and K 17 sts from other side of heel. K across first 11 heel sts.
1st round Work to end, keeping instep sts in patt and rem sts in stockinette st.
2nd round First needle, K to last 3 sts, K2 tog, K1; 2nd needle, patt to end; 3rd needle, K1, K2 tog, K to end.
Rep these 2 rounds until 16 sts rem on each of first and 3rd needles. Cont straight until foot measures 5½in (14cm) from where sts were picked up at heel, dec 2 sts evenly across instep on last round.
Sl first 2 sts of 2nd needle onto end of first needle and last 2 sts of 2nd needle onto 3rd needle.
Shape toe
1st round First needle, K to last 3 sts, K2 tog, K1; 2nd needle, K1, K2 tog tbl, K to last 3 sts, K2 tog, K1; 3rd needle, K1, K2 tog tbl, K to end.
2nd and 3rd rounds K to end.
Rep these 3 rounds until 32 sts rem. K sts from first needle onto 3rd needle. Graft or bind off sts from 2 needles together.
Ruffle
Using size B (2.50mm) hook, B and with WS of work facing, work 50sc around top of sock. Work 5 rounds of sc.
Last round *1sc into next st, 1dc into next st, 1tr into each of next 2 sts, 1dc into next st, rep from * to end. Fasten off.

Black and white striped socks

Sizes
Foot length, 9½in (24cm).
Leg including heel, 16½in (42cm).

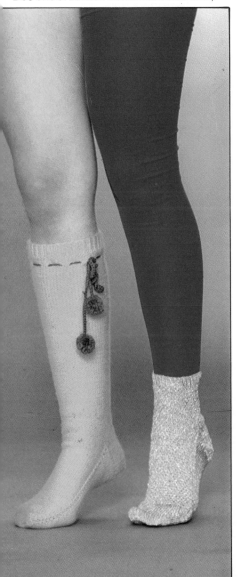

Materials

4oz (100g) of a sport yarn in main color (A)
2oz (50g) in contrasting color (B)
1 pair No. 2 (2¾mm) knitting needles

Gauge

32 sts and 42 rows to 4in (10cm) on No 2 (2¾mm) needles.

To make

Using No. 2 (2¾mm) needles and A, cast on 73 sts.
1st ribbing row K1, (P1, K1) to end.
2nd ribbing row P1, (K1, P1) to end.
Rep these 2 rows for 1in (2.5cm); end with a 2nd ribbing row.
Beg with a K row, cont in stockinette st working in stripes of 28 rows A and 28 rows B throughout until work measures 7in (18cm); end with a P row.

Shape leg

Dec one st at each end of next and every foll 8th row until 65 sts rem. Cont without shaping until work measures 13½in (34.5cm); end with a P row. Cut off yarn. Divide for instep and complete as for maroon socks, working toe and heel in main color.

Multi-colored striped socks

Sizes

Foot length, 9½in (24cm).
Leg including heel, 23½in (59.5cm).

Materials

4oz (100g) of a sport yarn in a plain color (A)
2oz (50g) in each of 2 contrasting plain colors (B and C)
2oz (50g) in each of 3 contrasting flecked colors (D, E and F)
1 set of four Nos. 2 and 4 (3 and 3¾mm) knitting needles

Gauge

24 sts and 34 rows to 4in (10cm) on No. 4 (3¾mm) needles.

To make

Using three of the set of No. 2 (3mm) needles and A, cast on 16 sts onto first and 2nd needles and 40 sts onto 3rd needle. Using 4th needle, work in rounds of K2, P2 ribbing for 2in (5cm). Change to set of No. 4 (3¾mm) needles. Cont in stockinette st, working stripe sequence of 15 rounds D, 15 rounds B, 15 rounds E, and 15 rounds C. Now work 7 rounds F.

Shape leg

Next round K to end, dec on 3rd needle thus: K17, sl 1, K1, psso, K2 then mark these 2 sts for center back, K2 tog, K17. 38 sts on 3rd needle.
Work 7 rounds F.
Dec one st each side of center 2 sts, as before, on next and every foll 8th row

6 times, work 29 rounds A, 15 rounds D and 15 rounds B. Now work 1 round E, dec as before. 24 sts on 3rd needle. Place 2 sts at beg of 1st needle and 2 sts at end of 2nd needle on 3rd needle. 28 sts on 3rd needle and 14 sts on 1st and 2nd needles.
Work 14 rounds E and 15 rounds C.

Shape heel

Cont to work on sts on 3rd needle only for heel, using A.
1st row K27, turn.
2nd row P26, turn.
3rd row K25, turn.
Cont to work 1 st less on every row until the row P6, turn has been worked.
Next row K6, pick up loop lying between needles and K it tog with next st, turn.
Next row P7, pick up loop lying between needles and P it tog with next st, turn.
Cont in this way until all sts are worked back onto one needle. 28 sts.
Next row K14, sl instep sts onto one needle.
Now using free needle cont in rounds: work 15 rounds F, 15 rounds A and 10 rounds D.

Shape toe

1st round Beg with 2nd needle, K to last 3 sts, K2 tog, K1, from 3rd needle K1, sl 1, K1, psso, K to last 3 sts, K2 tog, K1, then from first needle K1, sl 1, K1, psso, K to end.
2nd round K.
Rep these 2 rounds until 16 sts rem. K sts from 2nd needle onto first needle. Graft or bind off sts from 2 needles together.

Over-the-knee-socks with black foot

Sizes

Foot length, 9½in (24cm).
Leg including heel, 25in (64cm).

Materials

8oz (200g) of shaded knitting worsted in main color (A)

4oz (100g) of a knitting worsted in a contrasting color (B)
1 set of four Nos 2 and 5 (3 and 4mm) knitting needles

Gauge

20 sts and 28 rows to 4in (10cm) on No. 5 (4mm) needles.

To make

Using three of the set of four No. 5 (3mm) needles and B, cast on 16 sts onto first and 2nd needles and 32 sts onto 3rd needle. Using 4th needle, work in rounds of K2, P2 ribbing for 1½in (3.5cm). Cut off B. Change to the set of No. 5 (4mm) needles. Join on A and P1 row. The inside is now RS of work. Now K until work measures 10in (25.5cm) from beg.

Shape leg

Next round K to end, dec on 3rd needle thus: K13, sl 1, K1, psso, K2 then mark these 2 sts for center back, K2 tog, K to end. 30 sts on 3rd needle.
Dec one st at each side of center 2 sts, as before, on every foll 8th row 8 times in all. 16 sts on 3rd needle. Place 4 sts from beg of first needle and 4 sts from end of 2nd needle onto 3rd needle. 24 sts on 3rd needle and 12 sts on first and 2nd needles.
Cont without shaping until work measures 22½in (57cm) from beg.
Cut off A.
Join on B and P 3 rounds.

Shape heel

Turn work to RS and cont to work in stockinette st on sts on 3rd needle only

for heel.
1st row K23, turn.
2nd row P22, turn.
3rd row K21, turn.
Cont to work 1 st less on every row until the row P8, turn has been worked.
Next row K8, pick up loop lying between

needles and K it tog with next st, turn.
Next row K9, pick up loop lying between needles and K it tog with next st, turn.
Cont in this way until all sts are worked back onto one needle. 24 sts.
Place a marker at end of last row.
Next row K12, sl instep sts onto one needle.
Cont in stockinette st until foot measures 5½in (14cm) from marker.
Shape toe
1st round From first needle, K to last 3 sts, K2 tog, K1, from 2nd needle, K1, sl 1, K1, psso, K to last 3 sts, K2 tog, K1, from 3rd needle, K1, sl 1, K1, psso, K to end.
2nd round K.
Rep these 2 rounds until 16 sts rem. K sts from first needle onto 3rd needle. Graft or bind off sts from 2 needles together.

Yellow socks with pompom trim

Sizes
Foot length, 9½in (24cm).
Leg including heel, 15in (38cm).

Materials
6oz (150g) of a sport yarn in main color (A)
2oz (50g) in contrasting color for trim (B)
1 pair No. 3 (3¼mm) knitting needles
1 medium-sized crochet hook

Gauge
26 sts and 35 rows to 4in (10cm) on No. 3 (3¼mm) needles.

To make
Using No. 3 (3¼mm) needles and A, cast on 65 sts.
1st ribbing row K1, (P1, K1) to end.
2nd ribbing row P1, (K1, P1) to end.
Rep these 2 rows for 1in (2.5cm); end with a 2nd ribbing row. Beg with a P row, cont in reverse stockinette st for 5 rows.
Eyelet hole row K1, *K1, yo, K2 tog, rep from * to last st, K1.
Beg with a P row, cont in reverse stockinette st until work measures 7in (18cm); end with a K row.
Shape leg
Dec one st at each end of next and every foll 6th row until 57 sts rem.
Cont straight until work measures 13½in (34.5cm); end with a K row.
Cut off yarn.
Divide for instep
Next row Sl first 14 sts onto a length of yarn, rejoin yarn to next st and work across center 29 sts, sl last 14 sts onto a length of yarn. Work in reverse stockinette st on center 29 sts for 5½in (14cm) for instep; end with a K row.
Shape toe
Dec one st at each end of next and every foll alternate row until 11 sts rem.
Bind off.

Join back seam.
Place 2 sets of 14 sts onto one needle. With RS facing join on yarn and work on these 28 sts for heel as foll:
1st row P13, sl 1, P1, psso, P to end. 27 sts.
2nd row K to end.
3rd row *Sl 1 purlwise, P1, rep from * to last 3 sts, sl 1 purlwise, P2.
Rep last 2 rows 11 times more, then work the 2nd row again.
Turn heel
1st row P17, P2 tog, turn.
2nd row K8, K2 tog, turn.
3rd row P8, P2 tog, turn.
Rep last 2 rows until all sts have been worked ending with a 2nd row. 9 sts.
Next row (RS) P9, pick up 14 sts along side of heel.
Next row K23, pick up 14 sts along other side of heel. 37 sts.
Cont in reverse stockinette st, dec one st at each end of next and every foll alternate row until 29 sts rem. Cont straight until work measures same as instep to toe shaping; end with a K row.
Shape toe
Dec one st at each end of next and every foll alternate row until 11 sts rem. Bind off.

To finish
Join foot seams.

Ties
Using crochet hook and contrasting yarn make 2 chains, each 36in (91cm) long. Thread one tie through eyelet holes of each sock. Make 4 pompoms and sew one to each end of ties.

Silver socks

Sizes
Foot length, 8½in (22cm).
Leg including heel, 6¾in (17cm).

Materials
2oz (40g) of a sport-weight metallic yarn
1 set of four No. 2 (2¾mm) double-pointed knitting needles

Gauge
44 sts and 44 rows to 4in (10cm) on No. 2 (2¾mm) needles.

To make
Using 3 of set of four No. 2 (2¾mm) needles cast on 28sts onto first needle and 24sts onto 2nd and 3rd needles.
Using 4th needle work in rounds of K1, P1 ribbing for 1in (2.5cm). Beg patt.
1st and 2nd rounds *P1, K1, rep from * to end.
3rd and 4th rounds *K1, P1 rep from * to end.
These 4 rounds form patt. Cont in patt until work measures 4in (10cm).
Shape heel
Next row K18, sl last 18sts of round onto other end of same needle; these 36sts are for the heel.
Divide rem 40sts onto 2 needles and leave for instep. Beg with a P row, work 27 rows stockinette st on 36sts for heel.
Turn heel
1st row K22, K2 tog, turn.
2nd row P9, P2 tog, turn.
3rd row K10, K2 tog, turn.
Cont in this way until all sts are on one needle.

Next row K11, so completing heel.
Sl all instep sts onto one needle. Using one free needle K rem 11 heel sts, pick up and K 17sts from side of heel, patt across instep sts, using another free needle pick up and K 17sts from other side of heel, then K rem 11 heel sts.
Mark end of last row.
Working instep sts in patt and rem sts in stockinette st, shape foot as foll:
1st round Work to end.
2nd round K to last 3 sts on first needle, K2 tog, K1, work across sts on 2nd needle, K1, K2 tog tbl, K to end of sts on 3rd needle.
Rep these 2 rounds until 16sts rem on each of first and 3rd needles. Cont without shaping until foot measures 5½in (14cm) from marker. Sl first 2 sts from 2nd needle onto end of first needle and last 2 sts on 2nd needle onto 3rd needle.

Shape toe

1st round K to last 3 sts on first needle, K2 tog, K1, from 2nd needle K1, K2 tog tbl, K to last 3 sts, K2 tog, K1, from 3rd needle K1, K2 tog tbl, K to end.
2nd and 3rd rounds K.
Rep these 3 rounds until 32 sts rem. K sts from first needle onto 3rd needle. Bind off sts from both needles together.

Gold socks

Sizes

Foot length, 8½in (22cm).
Leg including heel, 6¾in (17cm).

Materials

2oz (40g) of a sport-weight metallic yarn
1 set of four No. 2 (2¾mm) double-pointed knitting needles

Gauge

45 sts and 48 rows to 4in (10cm) on No. 2 (2¾mm) needles.
To make
Using 3 of set of four No. 2 (2¾mm) needles cast 28 sts onto first needle and 24 sts onto 2nd and 3rd needles. Using 4th needle work in rounds of K1, P1 ribbing for 1in (2.5cm). Beg patt.
1st round P.
2nd round *K1, P1, rep from * to end.

These 2 rounds form patt. Cont in patt until work measures 4in (10cm) from beg.
Shape heel
Next row P18, sl last 18 sts of round onto other end of same needle; these 36 sts are for the heel.
Divide rem 40 sts onto 2 needles and leave for instep. Beg with a K row, work 27 rows reverse stockinette st on 36 sts for heel.
Turn heel
1st row P22, P2tog, turn.
2nd row K9, K2 tog, turn.
3rd row P10, P2tog, turn.
Cont in this way until all sts are on one needle. 22 sts.
Next row P11, so completing heel.
Sl all instep sts onto one needle. Using one free needle P rem 11 heel sts, pick up and K 17 sts from side of heel, patt across instep sts, using another free needle pick up and K 17 sts from other side of heel, then P rem 11 heel sts.
Mark end of last row.

Working instep sts in patt and rem sts in reverse stockinette st shape foot as foll:
1st round Work to end.
2nd round P to last 3 sts on 1st needle, P2 tog, P1, work across sts on 2nd needle, P1, P2 tog tbl, P to end of sts on 3rd needle.
Rep these 2 rounds until 16 sts rem on each of first and 3rd needles. Cont without shaping until foot measures 5½in (14cm) from marker.
Sl first 2 sts from 2nd needle onto end of first needle and last 2 sts on 2nd needle onto 3rd needle.
Shape toe
1st round P to last 3 sts on first needle, P2 tog, P1, from 2nd needle P1, P2 tog tbl, P to last 3 sts, P2 tog, P1, from 3rd needle P1, P2tog tbl, P to end.
2nd and 3rd rounds P.
Rep these 3 rounds until 32 sts rem. P sts from first needle onto 3rd needle. Bind off sts from both needles together.

Dotted socks

Sizes

Foot length, 9½in (24cm).
Leg including heel, 16in (40.5cm).

Materials

4oz (100g) of a sport yarn in main color (A)
2oz (50g) in contrasting color (B)
1 pair each Nos. 00 and 2 (2mm and 2¾mm) knitting needles
1 set of four No. 2 (2¾mm) double-pointed knitting needles

Gauge

31 sts and 44 rows to 4in (10cm) on No. 2 (2¾mm) needles.

To make
Divide B into several small balls for dots.
Using pair of No. 00 (2mm) needles and A, cast on 86 sts. Work in K2, P2 ribbing for 1½in (4cm). Change to pair of No. 2 (2¾mm) needles. Beg dot patt.

1st row K10 A, join on one ball of B, 5 B, 38 A, join on a second ball of B, 5 B, 28 A.
2nd row P26 A, 9 B, 34 A, 9 B, 8 A.
3rd row K7 A, 11 B, 32 A, 11 B, 25 A.
4th row P24 A, 13 B, 30 A, 13 B, 6A.
5th row K6 A, 13 B, 30 A, 13 B, 24 A.
6th row As 4th.
7th-11th rows Work 5th-1st rows in this order.
These 11 rows form the dots.
Cont in stockinette st, placing dots at random by altering the number of sts and rows between each dot (we have worked 13 dots over sock) until work measures 3in (8cm). Inc one st at each end of next and every foll 8th row until there are 92 sts. Now dec one st at each end of next and every foll 8th row to 72 sts. Cont without shaping until work measures 13¾in (35cm); end with a P row.
Cut off yarn.
Divide for heel
Sl the first 20 sts onto one of the set of four needles, sl next 32 sts onto a holder for instep and the last 20 sts onto another of the set of four needles.
With RS facing join yarn to sts on 2nd needle, K20, then K20 from first needle. (Leg seam is now in center of work.)
P1 row on these 40 sts. Mark end of last row.
Turn heel
1st row K39.
Turn.
2nd row P38.
Turn.
3rd row K37.
Turn.
4th row P36.
Turn.
Cont to work one st less on every row until the row P12, turn has been worked.
Next row K12, pick up loop lying between needles and K it tog with next st, turn.
Next row P13, pick up loop lying between needles and P it tog with next st, turn.
Cont in this way until all sts are on one needle, 40 sts.
Shape foot
Dec one st at each end of next and every foll alternate row until 32 sts rem. Cont straight until work measures 7in (17.5cm) from marker; end with a P row.
Shape toe
1st row K2, sl 1, K1, psso, K to last 4 sts, K2 tog, K2.
2nd row P.
Rep these 2 rows until 14 sts rem. Cut off yarn.
Return to sts on holder, join on yarn and cont in stockinette st until instep is same length as foot to beg of toe shaping.
Shape toe
1st row K2, sl 1, K1, psso, K to last 4 sts, K2 tog, K2.
2nd row P.
Rep these 2 rows until 14 sts rem. Graft or bind off the 2 sets of sts together. Join leg and foot seams.

KNITTING

Striped classic

Bouclé yarn makes a classic jacket in a subtle blend of colors to wear with many different outfits.

Sizes
To fit 32½[34:36:38:40]in (83[87:92: 97:102]cm) bust
Length, 25½[26:26½:27:27½]in (65[66: 67:69:70]cm)
Sleeve seam, 17in (43cm).
Note Directions for larger sizes are in brackets [ ] ; if there is only one set of figures it applies to all sizes.

Materials
8[9:9:11:11]oz (200[250:250: 300:300]g) of a lightweight bouclé yarn in 1st color (A)

Ross Greetham

8[8:8:9:9]oz (200[200:200:250:
250]g) in 2nd color (B)
6[6:6:8:8]oz (150[150:150:200]g)
in 3rd color (C)
1 pair each Nos. 4 and 6(3¾ and
4½mm) knitting needles

Gauge
18sts to 4in (10cm) over rev stockinette
stitch worked on No. 6 (4½mm) needles.

Pocket linings (make 2)
Using No. 6 (4½mm) needles and C, cast
on 26sts.
Beg with a P row, cont in rev stockinette
st working in stripes of 2 rows C,
2 rows B and 2 rows A, until the 5th
B stripe has been worked. Cut off yarn
and leave sts on a holder.

Right front
Using No. 4 (3¾mm) needles and A, cast
on 55[57:59:61:63] sts. K7 rows.
Inc row K3[4:5:6:7], (inc in next st,
K9) 4 times, inc in next st, K to last 7 sts,
sl these 7 sts on a safety-pin for front
border. 53[55:57:59:61] sts. ** Change
to No. 6 (4½mm) needles. Beg with a P
row cont in rev stockinette st in stripes of
2 rows C, 2 rows B and 2 rows A until the
2nd B stripe has been worked.
Cont in stripe sequence shape as foll:
Dec row P to last 10 sts, P3 tog, P7.
Work 9 rows.
Rep last 10 rows once more, then work
the dec row again. 47[49:51:53:55] sts.
Work 3 rows.
Pocket row P14[15:16:17:18], sl next
26 sts on a holder; in their place P sts
of one pocket lining, P to end of row.
Cont straight until work measures
10½in (27cm); end with a K row.
Shape front edge
Dec one st at front edge on next and
every foll 4th row until 35[37:39:41:43]
sts rem, then on foll 6th row. 34[36:38:
40:42] sts. Work 4 rows straight;
end at side edge.
Shape armhole
Bind off 7[8:9:10:11] sts at beg of next
row.**
Dec one st at front edge on next and foll
6th row, at the same time dec one st at
armhole edge on next and every foll
alternate row. 21[22:23:24:25] sts.
Keeping armhole edge straight, cont to
dec at front edge on every foll 6th row
until 17[17:18:18:19] sts rem. Cont
straight until armhole measures 7[7½:8:
8¼:8½]in (18[19:20:21:22]cm); end
at armhole edge.
Shape shoulder
Cast off 6 sts at beg of next and foll
alternate row. Work 1 row. Bind off.

Left front
Using No. 4 (3¾mm) needles and A, cast
on 55[57:59:61:63] sts. K7 rows.
Inc row K7, sl these sts on a safety-pin, K4
[5:6:7:8], (inc in next st, K9) 4 times, inc
in next st, K to end. 53[55:57:59:61] sts.

Now work as right front from ** to **
noting that dec row will read P7, P3 tog,
P to end and pocket row will read
P7[8:9:10:11], sl next 26 sts on a holder
and in their place P the sts of pocket
lining, P to end of row. K1 row, then
complete as right front.

Back
Using No. 4 (3¾mm) needles and A, cast
on 81[85:89:93:97] sts. K7 rows.
Inc row K4[6:8:10:12], (inc in next st,
K7) 9 times, inc in next st, K to end.
91[95:99:103:107] sts.
Change to No. 6 (4½mm) needles. Beg
with a P row, cont in rev stockinette st
working in stripes of 2 rows C, 2 rows B
and 2 rows A until the 2nd B stripe has
been worked. Cont in stripe sequence
shape as foll:
Dec row P7, P3 tog, P to last 10 sts,
P3 tog, P7. Work 9 rows. Rep last 10 rows
until 79[83:87:91:95] sts rem. Cont
straight until back measures same as fronts
to beg of armholes; end with a K row.
Shape armholes
Bind off 7[8:9:10:11] sts at beg of next
2 rows. Dec one st at each end of next
and foll 3 alternate rows. 57[59:61:63:
65] sts. Cont straight until armholes are
same depth as front armholes to beg
of shoulder shaping; end with a K row.
Shape shoulders
Bind off 6 sts at beg of next 4 rows and 5
[5:6:6:7] sts at beg of foll 2 rows. Bind off.

Sleeves
Using No. 4 (3¾mm) needles and A, cast
on 39[41:43:45:47] sts. K8 rows inc
4 sts evenly on last row. 43[45:47:49:
51] sts. Change to No. 6 (4½mm) needles.
Beg with a P row, cont in rev stockinette
st inc one st at each end of 13th and every
foll 12th row until there are 59[61:63:65:
67] sts. Cont straight until sleeve measures

17in (43cm) from beg; end with same
color stripe to match left front.
Shape top
Bind off 7[8:9:10:11] sts at beg of next
2 rows. Dec one st at each end of next
and every foll 4th row until 37[35:31:
29:27] sts rem, then at each end of every
foll alternate row until 23 sts rem, then
on every row until 17 sts rem. Bind off.

Pocket tops (alike)
With RS facing, using No. 4 (3¾mm)
needles and A, K sts from holder. K6
rows. Bind off.

Right front border and collar
Join shoulder seams. Place the 7 sts of
right front on a No. 6 (4½mm) needle with
point at inner end. Join on yarn and work
in garter st until border, slightly stretched,
fits up front edge to beg of front shaping.
Shape collar by inc one st at inner edge
on next and every foll 4th row until there
are 12 sts, then on every foll 6th row until
there are 17 sts, then on every 8th row
until there are 22 sts. Cont straight until
shaped edge of collar, slightly stretched,
fits up to shoulder, ending on RS.
Next row K to last 4 sts, turn.
Next row Sl 1, K to end.
Work 2 rows across all sts.
Rep these 4 rows 3 times more.
Cont straight until collar fits around to
center back neck. Bind off.

Left front border and collar
Work as right front border and collar but
work 1 row less before turning rows.

To finish
Press or block, according to yarn used.
Set in sleeves. Join side and sleeve seams.
Sew down pocket linings and ends of
pocket tops. Sew on borders and collar,
joining bound-off edges at back of neck.

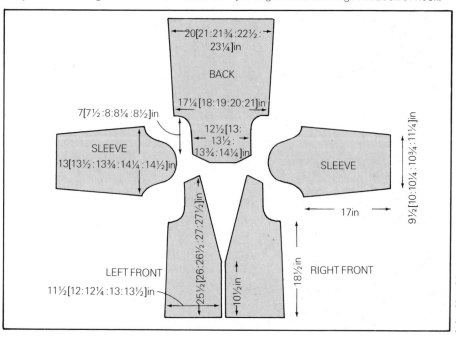

SEWING

Soft and sultry

Light and airy, this blouse has an elasticized neckline that can be worn on or off the shoulder. The skirt is cut as a swinging half circle with a pretty ruffled hem.

Blouse

Measurements
To fit small and average sizes.
Finished length of blouse, 22¾in (58cm).

Suggested fabrics
Voile, cheesecloth, seersucker, chambray. For the embroidered version, evenweave cotton or voile.

Jean-Claude Volpelière

Materials

2⅝yd (2.3m) of 36in (90cm)-wide or
1⅜yd (1.2m) of 60in (150cm)-wide
fabric
Matching thread, round elastic,
bodkin
For embroidered version: Stranded
embroidery floss, crewel needle,
yardstick, tailor's chalk, flexible
curve

1 Mark the pattern pieces on the
fabric, using tailor's chalk, yardstick and
flexible curve for marking neckline.
2 Cut two bodice pieces and two sleeves.
⅝in (1.5cm) seam allowances are
included. Mark underarm points on
bodice and sleeves with tailor's tacks.

3 Matching underarm points, pin, baste
and stitch sleeves to back and front bodice
along shoulder seams. French seams will
provide a neat finish. Press seams.

4 Join sleeve underarm seams and side
seams in one operation, pivoting machine
needle at underarm points and using
French seams. Press.
5 On the neck edge turn under and press
a ¼in (6mm) hem. Turn under a further
¾in (2cm), baste and stitch along basted
edge. Stitch another line ¼in (6mm)
above the first to form a casing for the
elastic. Sew a small eyelet at center
front on the wrong side for the elastic.
Stitch sleeve hems, making casings for
elastic in the same way.

Jean-Claude Volpelière

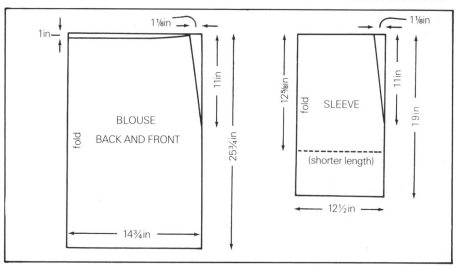

BLOUSE
BACK AND FRONT

1in

1⅛in

11in

25¾in

14¾in

fold

SLEEVE

1⅛in

12⅝in

11in

19in

(shorter length)

12½in

fold

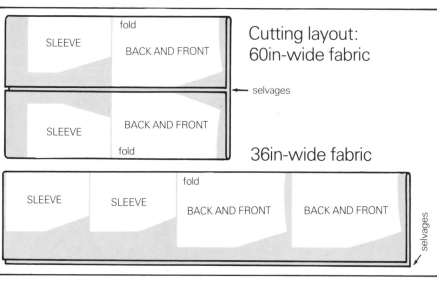

SLEEVE

fold

BACK AND FRONT

selvages

SLEEVE

BACK AND FRONT

fold

Cutting layout:
60in-wide fabric

36in-wide fabric

SLEEVE

SLEEVE

fold

BACK AND FRONT

BACK AND FRONT

selvages

John Hutchinson

6 Turn under and stitch a $\frac{3}{8}$in (1cm) deep double hem at lower edge of blouse.
7 Using a bodkin thread elastic around neck. Pull up to measure about 36in (90cm) all around. Cut off elastic leaving several inches for adjusting length and knot ends temporarily. Try on blouse and check that neckline is comfortable when pulled off the shoulders.
8 Trim ends of elastic and overcast together securely. Thread elastic through lower edges of sleeves, check fit and anchor ends.

Embroidered version

Cut out and make as for elasticized version but embroider center front before pulling up neckline (see Technique tip). Sleeves can be made the shorter length shown on the measurement diagram and hemmed at the bottom.

Technique tip

Cross stitch

This should be worked on an evenweave fabric on which threads can be counted easily, making it possible to produce neat, identical stitches. Ideally, each stitch should fill a perfect square if worked down and across an even number of threads.

Start by working all the stitches in one direction, working down the fabric from the neckline. The needle should pass horizontally across the fabric.

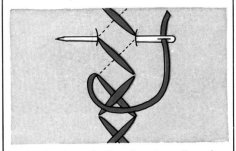

Work back up the line, forming a line of crosses. You may find it easier to make the stitches even if you mark the lines with two rows of basting first.

Cutting layout:
36in-wide fabric

fold

selvages

RUFFLE

RUFFLE

WAISTBAND

SKIRT
BACK AND FRONT

selvages

54/60in-wide fabric

selvages

SKIRT
BACK AND FRONT

fold

selvages

RUFFLE
(single layer)

WAISTBAND

RUFFLE

selvages

John Hutchinson

Skirt

Measurements
To fit small and medium sizes.
Finished length of skirt, 29in (73.5cm).
Directions are given for cutting the skirt to fit any waist size.

Suggested fabrics
Plain cottons or those with small all-over patterns. Stripes and plaids are unsuitable; they will run in different directions at the seams. If using border fabric, check layout and allow extra fabric.

Materials
3yd (2.7m) of 36in (90cm)-wide or 2½yd (2.2m) of 54/60in (40/150m)-wide fabric
Matching thread, 8in (20cm) zipper
4in (10cm) of 36in (90cm)-wide interfacing for waistband
2 hooks and eyes
Yardstick
Tailor's chalk

1 Fold the fabric as shown in the cutting layout and pin the edges together. Mark the pattern pieces on the fabric using tailor's chalk and a yardstick.
2 To calculate the waist curve, take one third of your waist measurement, plus $1\frac{1}{4}$in (3cm) for seams – i.e. for a 25in (63cm) waist size the sum is $25+1\frac{1}{4}=26\frac{1}{4}$in (63+3=66cm). Divided by three= $8\frac{3}{4}$in (22cm). Measure the calculated amount – in this case $8\frac{3}{4}$in (22cm) – down from the top of the left-hand corner of the fabric. This will be the radius of the waist curve. Mark with chalk. Continue measuring this distance from the corner point of the fabric and marking with

chalk. Join the marks to form the waist curve. Measure around this curve to check that it is half your waist size, plus $1\frac{1}{4}$in (3cm). If it is too large, raise the line and re-mark until the result is correct. Before cutting out, draw another line $\frac{5}{8}$in (1.5cm) above waistline for waistband seam allowance.

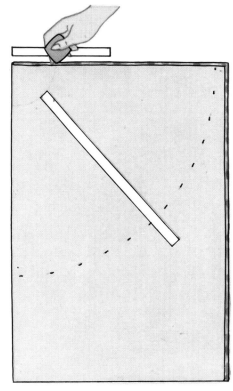

3 From the waist curve measure down $20\frac{3}{4}$in (52.5cm) and mark with chalk. Using your yardstick, continue measuring down at 2in (5cm) intervals along waist

curve to mark the parallel curve of the hem. Before cutting out, check finished length by adding 9in (23cm) for ruffle. Adjust the skirt length if necessary.

4 Cut out ruffle pieces, each 10¾in (27.5cm) wide, to make a total length of 4yd (3.6m) as shown in layouts.

5 For waistband cut a strip of fabric 3in (7.5cm) wide by waist measurement plus 2⅜in (6cm). Cut strip of interfacing to the same length and half the width.

6 With right sides together and raw edges even, pin, baste and stitch side seams of skirt, leaving 8¼in (21cm) open on left side seam for insertion of zipper. Staystitch around the waistline. Press seams open and finish.

7 Because of the bias cut of the skirt, the center back and front are likely to "drop," making the hem uneven. To correct this, leave the skirt hanging for several days. Pin the waist edges of the skirt together. Pin it onto loops of seam binding and suspend it from a hanger, or pin it to a dress form if you have one.

8 Insert zipper in side opening (see Volume 2, page 45). Interface waistband and attach to skirt (see Volume 2, page 50). Finish lower edge of skirt with zig-zag machine stitching or overcasting.

9 Join the short edges of the ruffle pieces with right sides together and raw edges even, to make a circle. Press seams open and finish. Turn up and stitch a ⅜in- (1cm)-deep double hem around one edge of ruffle and a ¼in- (6mm-) deep double hem around remaining edge of ruffle. Press.

10 Run a line of gathering stitches ¾in (2cm) from the narrower hem, which will form the ruffled heading. Pull up gathering threads until ruffle fits lower edge of skirt.

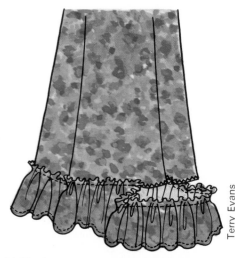

11 Pin the wrong side of the ruffle to the right side of the skirt, placing it ¼in (6mm) above the finished edge of the skirt. Topstitch ruffle to skirt along the line of gathering. Finish waistband with hooks and eyes.

EXTRA SPECIAL **SEWING**

Bare essentials

Here is a dress with a beautifully bared back, which can be an apron, a jumper or an evening dress.

Victor Yuan

Measurement diagram

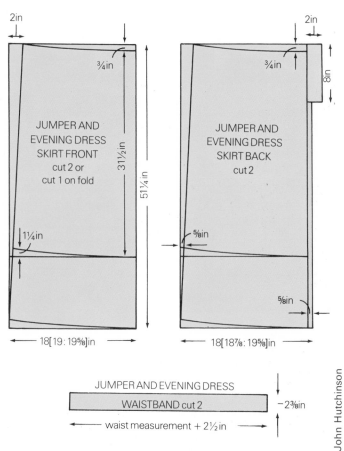

2in	2in
¾in	¾in
	8in

JUMPER AND
EVENING DRESS
SKIRT FRONT
cut 2 or
cut 1 on fold

31½in

51¼in

1¼in

18[19 : 19⅝]in

JUMPER AND
EVENING DRESS
SKIRT BACK
cut 2

⅝in

⅝in

18[18⅞ : 19⅝]in

JUMPER AND EVENING DRESS

WAISTBAND cut 2   — 2⅜in

waist measurement + 2½ in

John Hutchinson

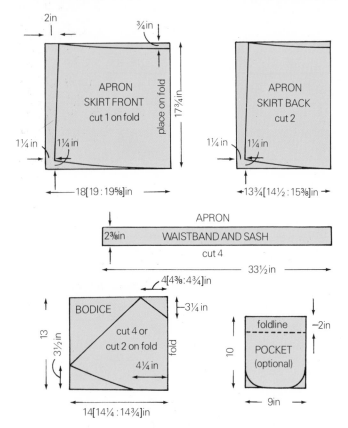

2in

¾ in

APRON
SKIRT FRONT
cut 1 on fold

place on fold

17¾in

1¼ in   1¼ in

18[19 : 19⅝]in

APRON
SKIRT BACK
cut 2

1¼ in   1¼ in

13¾[14½ : 15⅜]in

APRON

2⅜in   WAISTBAND AND SASH
cut 4

33½ in

4[4⅜ : 4¾]in

BODICE

3¼ in

13   cut 4 or
cut 2 on fold

3½ in   fold

4¼ in

14[14¼ : 14¾]in

foldline   —2in

POCKET
(optional)

10

9in

Cutting layout for 36in-wide fabric

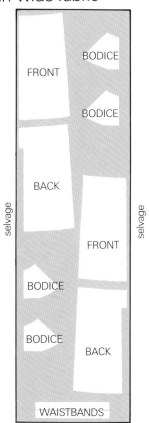

60in-wide fabric

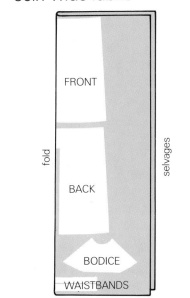

Measurements
To fit sizes 10 to 14. Finished length of skirt: apron, 15in (38.5cm); short, 27in (68.5cm); long, 37in (93.5cm).
Note: Measurements are given for size 10. Figures for larger sizes are given in brackets []. If only one figure is given, it applies to all sizes.

Suggested fabrics
Cotton, knits, silk, crepe or wool.

Materials
 60in (150cm)-wide fabric: apron, 1⅝yd (1.5m); short, 2½yd (2.2m); long, 3½yd (3.2m) or
 36in (90cm)-wide fabric: apron, 2⅜yd (2.1m); short, 3¾yd (3.4m); long, 6yd (5.5m)
 ⅛yd (.1m) of 36in (90cm)-wide interfacing
 Five ⅝in (1.5cm)-diameter buttons (or 2 for apron)
 Yardstick, tailor's chalk
 Flexible curve
 Matching thread, 1⅜yd (1.2m) woven tape

Evening dress and knee-length version

1 Mark the pattern pieces on the fabric using tailor's chalk, yardstick and flexible curve, following the appropriate measurement diagram and cutting layout. Cut out two complete bodice sections (bodice is made double). Cut out two waistbands, each a straight strip 2⅜in (6cm) wide by your waist measurement plus 2½in (6.5cm). Cut one waistband in interfacing. Cut out front skirt, then use it as a pattern for the back skirt. Place it on fabric still folded down center front as shown on 60in (150cm) fabric layout. Mark all around with tailor's chalk, adding 2in (5cm) by 8in (20cm) extension for buttons and ⅝in (1.5cm) seam allowance down center back.
Note: If using 36in (90cm)-wide fabric seam front skirt and bodice sections at center front. Add ⅝in (1.5cm) for these seams. ⅝in (1.5cm) has been included for other seams and 2in (5cm) for hem.
2 For shoulder straps, cut bias strips 2in (4cm) wide by about 27½in (70cm) for each strap. Cut pocket if required. Mark center front of bodice and skirt with tailor's tacks.

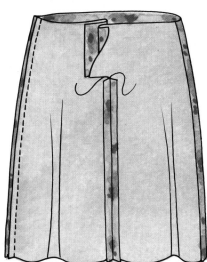

3 With right sides together and raw edges matching, pin, baste and stitch side

seams of skirt. Stitch center front seam if necessary. Stitch center back seam from button extension to hem. Press seams open and finish them. At lower end of button extension, clip right-hand seam allowance, press extension to one side, then fold in half as shown.
4 Baste interfacing to wrong side of one waistband piece. Join bias strips to make tubing for shoulder straps at least 27½in (70cm) long.

5 If using 36in (90cm)-wide fabric, stitch center front seam of each bodice section and press open. With right sides together and raw edges matching, pin, baste and stitch bodice sections together. Position straps at each point of bodice, enclosing them between the right sides of bodice, raw edges matching. Starting at lower edge, stitch to within ⅝in (1.5cm) of point, pivot needle and continue, stitching other corners the same way. Trim seam allowances, clip into center point of neckline and trim corners. Turn right side out and press.

6 Run a line of basting stitches all around bodice seam to hold it in position. Measure 2in (5cm) each side of center front and mark with a pin. Measure 6in (15cm) in from each side seam and mark again. Run a line of gathering stitches between each pair of pins and pull up thread until gathered sections each measure 2⅜in (6cm). Secure threads temporarily by winding them around pins.

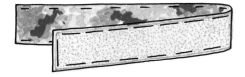

7 Fold waistband pieces so that one half is 1⅜in (3.5cm) longer than the other. Mark folds with pins to indicate center front of waistbands.

John Hutchinson

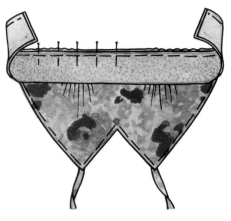

8 Matching centers of bodice and waistbands, enclose bodice between right sides of waistband pieces with interfaced section on top. With raw edges even, pin and baste.

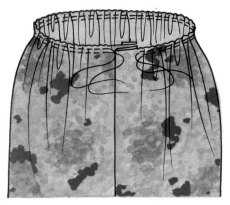

9 Run two lines of gathering stitches within seam allowance of skirt on waist edge, leaving button extensions free. Pull up gathers to fit waist, distributing fullness evenly, and secure threads.

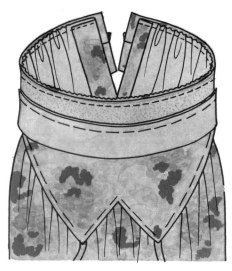

10 With interfacing upward, centers matching and right sides together, pin and baste remaining long edge of top waistband to skirt. Turn in and press seam allowance along free edge of inner waistband and baste to front waistband, enclosing top of skirt.

11 Try on dress and check fit of bodice gathers, bodice positioning and length needed for shoulder straps. When satisfied, rip out basting holding waistband to skirt.

12 Secure bodice gathers and stitch bodice to waistband. Trim interfacing close to stitching line. Trim seam allowances, turn waistbands downward and press.

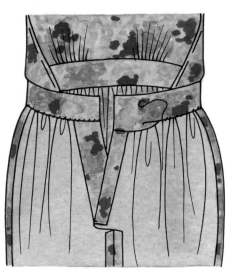

13 Rebaste long edge of top waistband to skirt as in step 10 and stitch. Trim seam allowances and press waistband. Slip stitch free edge of waistband over seamline on inside of skirt.

14 Turn in ends of waistband and slip stitch. Lap the folded half of button extension over opposite side and overcast ends on inside. Finish raw edges. Make two buttonholes, by hand or machine, in extension and one in waistband (see Volume 4, pages 56 and 57). Sew on three buttons to correspond. Turn up and sew hem. Sew ⅝in (1.5cm) loops at free ends of straps as shown. Sew buttons to fasten inside back edges of bodice.

Apron

1 Cut out pattern pieces, as described for evening and knee-length versions, but omit button allowance and add two extra waistband pieces for sash. Make as previously described, but do not stitch back seam. Turn under ⅜in (1cm) double hem down back edges.

2 Attach waistband as previously described. Draw up skirt so that finished back edge matches edge of bodice. Attach remaining waistband pieces to make a sash to tie at the back. Turn in seam allowances all around edges of sash; pin, baste and topstitch close to fold. Continue topstitching around upper and lower edges of waistband to finish.
3 Finish hem, attach button for straps and make up shoulder straps as for other versions.

Pocket (optional)

1 The pocket may be added to any version of the dress, either centered on the bodice or skirt, or positioned to one side of the skirt. Cut out the pocket piece, following the measurement diagram.
2 Finish the upper edge. Turn under and baste hem all around lower edges. Turn down top along foldline. Pin, baste and topstitch pocket to dress, centering it on the bodice or positioning it 1⅝in (4cm) from waist, either in the middle or half way between center front and side seam.

Homemaker

Paul Williams

Smocked accessories

Smocking is fun to do and will brighten up any room in the house. To make it even simpler, use a brightly-colored gingham, which makes the preparation quick and easy.

Choosing a design

Smocking designs are based on a combination of stitches, although a single-stitch design can also be effective. Remember that smocking stitches vary not only in appearance but also in degrees of elasticity and ease of working, so bear these factors in mind when planning a design.

Thread and needles

We used six strands of stranded embroidery floss on both the curtains and the pillows. Use a smooth needle with a sharp point. A crewel needle is best for use on long stitches. Remember that the size and type of needle depend on the fabric and the effect you want to achieve.

Making the gathers

1 Using a piece of strong synthetic thread, long enough to complete a row, across the fabric; work separate lines of gathering.
2 Start at the right-hand side of the fabric and sew with the wrong side of the fabric facing. Secure the thread with a knot and a backstitch, as a single knot might slip through the fabric when the gathers are pulled up.

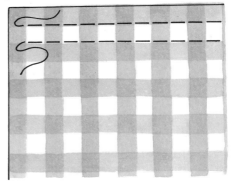

3 When gathering gingham, you can use either of two different methods. In the first method, used on the curtains, pass the needle under the right-hand corner of each gingham check, just picking it up. Leave remainder of thread hanging at left-hand side. This method needs fabric at least one and a half times finished width.

4 In the second method, used on the pillow, pass the needle under and over each gingham check in turn, until you reach the end . This method needs fabric at least three times the finished width.
5 When working either method, use a separate thread for each line and gather each row along the line between checks.
6 When you have completed the number of rows needed for your pattern, pull up the loose threads hanging at the left-hand side evenly but not too tightly, so that you can get the needle between the pleats when smocking.

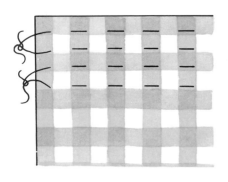

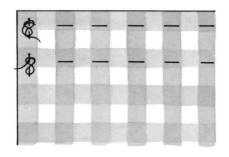

7 Either knot the loose ends together in pairs and cut off the excess thread, or place a pin in the left-hand margin and wind the threads around it. This second method permits you to adjust the threads if the gathering is too tight or too loose when the smocking is completed.
8 Turn the fabric right side up, ready for smocking. You will find that the lines of gathering will also act as a guide in keeping the rows of smocking stitches straight.

Finishing

1 When the smocking is complete, leave the gathering threads in place, lay the fabric wrong side up and press it lightly with a steam iron or a hot dry iron and a damp cloth. The steam sets the pleats and gives the work an even appearance.
2 Remove the gathering and assemble the item.

Smocked curtains

Finished size
To fit a window 48in (122cm) wide with a 39½in (100cm) drop, so each completed curtain measures 39½ × 24in (100 × 61cm).

Materials
3¾yd (3.5m) of 45in (115cm)-wide gingham
1⅜yd (1.2m) of 1⅛in (3cm)-wide Conso® shirring tape
¼yd (.2m) of 36in (90cm)-wide soft iron-on interfacing
Matching sewing thread
Three skeins of stranded embroidery floss

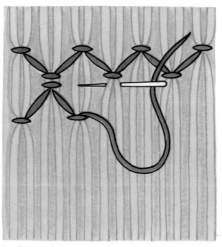

Diamond stitch

Bring the needle up to the left of the first pleat on the first row of gathering. With thread above the needle take a back-stitch through second pleat. Then go down to second row of gathering and take a backstitch through third pleat; repeat on fourth pleat with thread below the needle. Take needle up to left of fifth pleat on top row and repeat the process as from first pleat. Complete the line. This forms the first stage of the stitch. For the second stage, start on the third row of gathering so that the upper row of stitches is immediately above bottom stitches of the first row and work as for first stage. When diamond is complete, two pleats should lie in the center.

1 Cut the gingham into three 45in (115cm) lengths, making sure that the checks match.

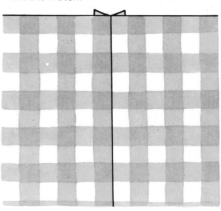

2 Cut one piece in half lengthwise. Pin each half to the outer edge of a full width, right sides facing and checks matching. Baste and stitch ⅜in (1cm) from selvages.

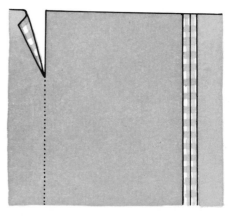

3 Open out fabric and press seam open. Measure 5in (13cm) from unseamed edge of narrow width and cut away the surplus fabric, cutting down a row of checks. (Wrong side shown plain.)
4 Repeat with remaining curtain panel.
5 From iron-on interfacing cut four strips, each 30 × 2in (76 × 5cm).

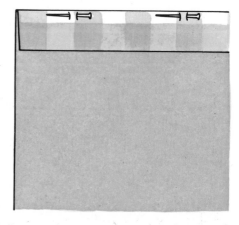

6 Fold 2¾in (7cm) to the wrong side of top of one curtain. Pin and baste in place.

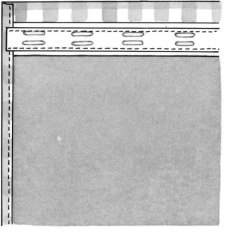

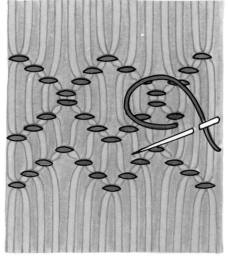

7 Place two interfacing strips, shiny down, on wrong side of curtain. Position each strip, 1½in (4cm) from top edge and ¾in (2cm) in from both side edges, butting the short edges of each strip together at the center. Iron strips in place.
8 Repeat steps 6 and 7 on other curtain panel.
9 Make a ⅜in (1cm)-wide double hem at the side edges on each curtain piece. Pin, baste and stitch in place.

10 At the lower edge of each curtain piece, turn up ¾in (2cm) and then a further 2in (5cm). Pin, baste and hem.
11 Begin the gathering for the smocking on the wrong side of one curtain, 1¼in (3cm) down from top edge, picking up only the right-hand corner of each check.
12 Work eight rows of gathering to a depth of about 2¾in (7cm), positioning each line along a row of checks. Pull up gathering threads so that panel measures 24in (61cm) in width and secure on the left-hand side.
13 Turn the curtain right side up. Using six strands of stranded embroidery floss and starting 1½in (4cm) from the top, work five single rows of diamond stitch.
14 When smocking is complete, press the smocked area on the wrong side. Remove the gathering threads.
15 Cut curtain tape into two lengths of 24¾in (63cm) each.

16 Turn under ⅜in (1cm) at each end of one curtain tape length. Pin tape in place on wrong side of curtain, with top edge of tape 2in (5cm) down from top edge of curtain. Hem tape in place.
17 Repeat steps 11-16 on other panel.

Pillows

Finished size
The pillows measure 12½in (32cm) square.
Materials for two pillows
  1⅝yd (1.4m) of 45in (115cm)-wide gingham
  ⅜yd (.3m) of 36in (90cm)-wide plain fabric
  Two skeins each of stranded embroidery floss in 3 matching and harmonizing colors, matching thread
  Two 12½in (32cm)-square pillow forms; alternatively, make your own pillow forms from unbleached muslin and polyester fiberfill

Surface honeycomb

Bring the needle up on the first pleat on the second gathering thread. Stitch this pleat and the next one together. Take another stitch over same pleats, take the needle down and bring it up at first gathering thread and stitch the second and third pleats together. Take the needle down to second gathering thread and stitch the third and fourth pleats together. Continue this pattern to the end of the row.

Trellis stitch

This stitch is worked in opposing zig-zag lines as shown in top drawing. Begin on first gathering thread and work down to second gathering thread over three or four pleats and up again over the same number of pleats. Keep the thread below the needle going up and above the needle going down. Slant the needle slightly, except at points where you should insert the needle horizontally. A single line of trellis (shown just below) is called wave stitch.

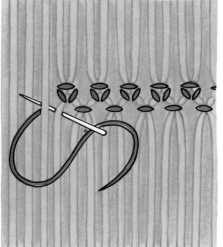

Vandyke stitch

Bring the needle up on the second pleat on the first gathering thread and back-stitch through the first and second pleats with the thread above the needle. Go down to the second gathering thread, pick up the second and third pleats and back stitch with the thread below the needle. Return to first gathering thread, connecting third and fourth pleats and backstitch with thread above the needle. Continue in this way to the end of the line.

Terry Evans

113

Colored smocked pillow

1 From gingham cut a piece for pillow front 10in (25cm) by width of fabric.
2 Work 20 rows of gathering horizontally across the pillow front, picking up alternate squares of gingham and leaving a $\frac{3}{4}$in (2cm) border on each selvage. Work the gathering so that when the gathers are pulled up the color of the gingham check will be predominant. Pull up the gathers and fasten off.
3 Turn the pillow front right side up. Work the rows of smocking stitches from the center outward.
4 In the center work three rows of surface honeycomb stitch in different colors, leaving a row of open checks between each row.
5 Leave a row of open checks, then work three rows of wave-type trellis stitch in different colors on each side.
6 Leave a row of open checks on each side, then work two rows of vandyke stitch on each side.

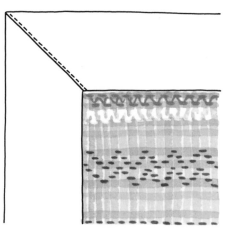

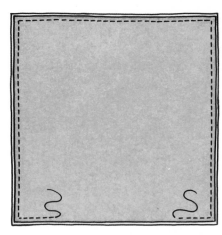

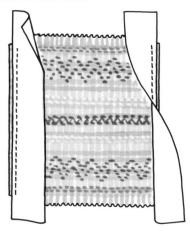

7 From plain fabric cut four strips, each $13\frac{3}{4} \times 2\frac{3}{4}$in (35 × 7cm). Pin, baste and stitch two strips down opposite sides of pillow front, each strip positioned $\frac{1}{4}$in (5mm) from smocking edge, with right sides together and taking a $\frac{3}{8}$in (1cm) seam on plain strip.
8 Pin, baste and stitch two remaining plain fabric strips across pillow front, $\frac{1}{4}$in (5mm) from end of smocking, taking

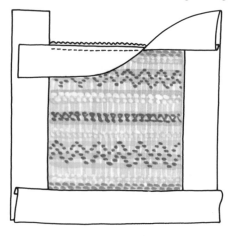

$\frac{3}{8}$in (1cm) seam on plain strip. At each corner, fold strips into a miter. Pin, baste and stitch in place on right side. Trim off excess gingham and excess strip fabric.
9 For ruffle, cut two $3\frac{1}{2}$in (9cm)-wide strips from the fabric width of the gingham. Pin, baste and stitch the two pieces together to form a ring, taking a $\frac{3}{8}$ to $\frac{3}{4}$in (1 to 2cm) seam, depending on matching checks. Trim and finish seams.

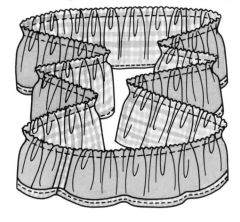

10 On one long edge of ruffle, turn under a double $\frac{1}{4}$in (5mm) hem. Pin, baste and stitch in place.
11 Run a line of gathering stitches along opposite long edge of ruffle, $\frac{3}{8}$in (1cm) from edge.

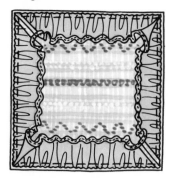

12 Pin ruffle around pillow front with right sides together, $\frac{3}{8}$in (1cm) from outer edge, pulling up gathering thread evenly to fit. Baste ruffle in place.
13 For back, cut a piece $13\frac{1}{4}$in (34cm) square from remaining gingham.

14 Place pillow back on pillow front, right sides together, with ruffle pointing inward, sandwiched between the two pieces. Pin, baste and stitch all around, taking a $\frac{3}{8}$in (1cm) seam and leaving an 8in (20cm) opening in one side. Clip corners and turn cover right side out.

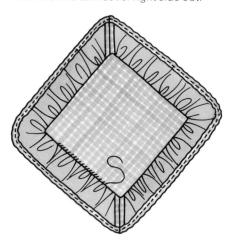

15 Insert pillow form. Turn in opening edges and slip stitch together to close.

White smocked pillow

1 Repeat steps 1 to 3 of colored smocked pillow, but pick up opposite squares in gathering so that when threads are pulled up the effect is white.
2 In the center of pillow front, work two rows of vandyke stitch in different colors.
3 Leave a row of open checks on each side, then work one row of wave stitch on each side of the center.
4 Leave a row of open checks on each side, then work two rows of surface honeycomb stitch, in different colors, with a row of open checks between each row.
5 Leave a row of open checks on each side, then work a row of vandyke stitch on each side.
6 Repeat steps 7 to 15 of colored smocked pillow to complete the white pillow.

Homemaker

Bed of roses

This fitted bedspread in a pretty border print will be the featured attraction in any bedroom.

DJ Lewis

Cutting layout: 48in-wide fabric

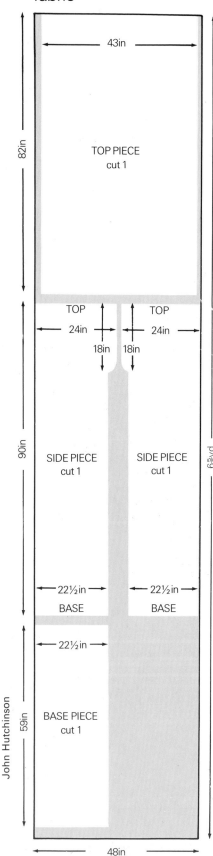

- 43in — TOP PIECE cut 1
- 82in
- 90in
- 59in
- TOP 24in / 18in — TOP 24in / 18in
- SIDE PIECE cut 1 — SIDE PIECE cut 1
- 22½in — 22½in
- BASE — BASE
- 22½in
- BASE PIECE cut 1
- 48in
- 6⅝yd

John Hutchinson

Size

To fit a twin bed, $39\frac{1}{2} \times 79$in (100×200cm). $\frac{3}{4}$in (2cm) seam allowances are included.

Materials

- $6\frac{5}{8}$yd (6m) of 48in (122cm)-wide border print fabric
- $6\frac{5}{8}$yd (6m) of 48in (122cm)-wide lining
- $1\frac{1}{8}$yd (1m) of 36in (90cm)-wide plain cotton fabric for cording
- 6yd (5.5m) filler cord; thread

1 Following the cutting plan, cut one top piece, one base piece and two side pieces from border print fabric. Graduate both side pieces as shown on cutting plan for the top edges.

2 Cut out the same pieces from lining, following the cutting plan.

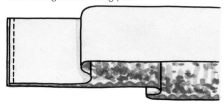

3 Using border fabric, right sides together and raw edges matching, pin, baste and stitch one side piece to the base piece down one short edge. Make sure that the edge of the border pattern is running along the lower edge of each piece so they will match.

4 Repeat to join short edge of second side piece to opposite edge of base piece.

5 Repeat steps 3 and 4 with lining pieces.

6 Place fabric side pieces and lining side pieces together, right sides facing and edges matching. Pin, baste and stitch along top side edges and lower edge. Trim seams and cut diagonally across the corners. Turn the complete side piece right side out, making sure the top corners are sharp.

7 Pin and baste the remaining long edges of fabric and lining side pieces together, matching edges.

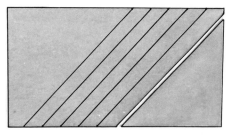

8 From cording fabric, cut out 2in (5cm)-wide strips on the bias. Pin, baste and stitch the strips together, right sides facing, to make a 6yd (5.5m)-long strip the same length as the filler cord.

9 Fold cording fabric around filler cord, wrong side inside. Pin and baste down complete length close to cord to hold it firmly in place.

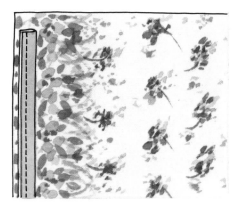

10 Pin the cording around the sides and base of the top fabric piece. Position the cording, starting $\frac{3}{4}$in (2cm) down from the top raw edge, with the cord facing in.

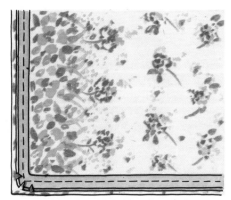

11 Curve the cording slightly around each corner, snipping into the cording fabric at each base corner to help it curve around easily. Baste and stitch the cording in place, leaving $\frac{3}{4}$in (2cm) free at both sides of the top edge, so the cording ends can be finished.

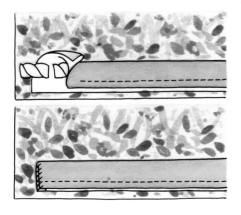

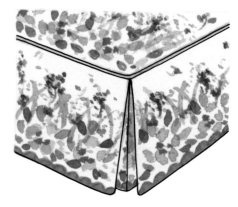

12 To finish the ends of the cording, remove stitching, peel back fabric from around the cord for ¾in (2cm) from the top edge. Cut off excess cord at this point. Trim and turn in the cording fabric; slip stitch the folded edges together.

13 Pin and baste the side piece around the fabric top, starting ¾in (2cm) down from top edge and matching side edge with end of cording. At each base corner, make a box pleat to give a tailored look to the bedspread.

14 Each corner pleat measures 8in (20cm) across, with the side seams centered on the corner at the back of each pleat. Stitch the side piece in place through all thicknesses, including the cording. Trim the fabric and press the seam toward the top piece. Turn the bedspread right side out and place it over the bed to check that the corners fit correctly.

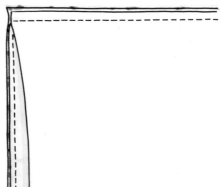

15 Place top lining on top fabric piece, with right sides together and top edges matching. Pin, baste and stitch across top edge, being careful not to catch in edges of cording or side piece.

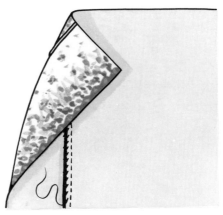

16 Turn under remaining raw edges all around lining top. Pin and baste. Fold lining down onto wrong side of fabric top, covering existing seam allowance. Pin, baste and hem in place on existing stitching line.

Di Lewis

Terry Evans

Homemaker

Jack and the beanstalk

Delight a child with this story quilt—as you tell the story you can make Jack really climb up the beanstalk.

Quilt

Finished size

65×43in (165×107cm). Suitable for twin bed, 79×40in (200×100cm). ¾in (2cm) seam allowances are included.

Materials

3⅜yd (3m) of 45in (115cm)-wide light blue heavyweight poplin
½yd (.4m) of 45in (115cm)-wide green heavyweight poplin
2yd (1.8m) of 45in (115cm)-wide red heavyweight poplin
3¾yd (3.4m) of 60in (152cm)-wide polyester batting
Scraps of cotton or cotton-blend fabrics including white fur fabric, dark brown corduroy, gold terrycloth and others as shown
One wooden bead
Scraps of flowery trimmings
Tracing paper; dressmaker's carbon
Matching sewing thread

1 For the background of the lower half of the picture, cut out a piece 32×12in (81×30cm) from green poplin.
2 For top of picture, cut out a piece 41×32in (104×81cm) from blue poplin.

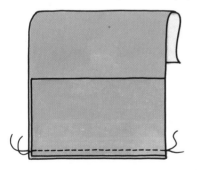

3 Place base and top pieces with right sides together, matching one 32in (81cm)-long edge. Pin, baste and stitch along this edge. Press seam open.

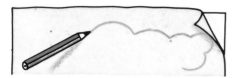

4 Trace the appliqué patterns from trace patterns on pages 123-125.

allowing ⅜in (1cm) extra where shown for appliqué overlap. Cut each piece in the appropriate fabric the number of times stated, omitting the leaves.

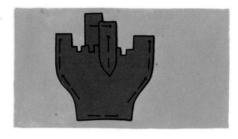

5 Position the castle on the background fabric, adding first the towers and then the turrets in numbered order. Pin in place.

6 From fur fabric, cut out one cloud shape, 15×6¼in (38×16cm). Pin to the background fabric, overlapping castle base.

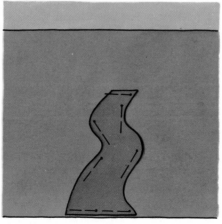

7 From brown corduroy, cut out a path 8¼in (21cm) long, curving it as shown. Pin in place on the background fabric.
8 Position the cottage walls on the background fabric, overlapping path. Pin firmly in place.

9 From light brown fabric cut out three 1¾in (4.5cm) squares for windowpanes. Using dark brown thread, stitch diagonally across each square of fabric to represent leaded panes. Place the panes behind the window frames, trimming off if necessary, and position them on cottage. Pin firmly in place.

10 Position door on cottage and pin firmly in place.

11 Position both roof pieces on top of cottage, overlapping walls. Pin in place.

12 From dark green fabric cut a bush 9 × 4¾in (23 × 12cm). Pin on background, overlapping cottage.

13 Work two lines of gray close zig-zag stitch from chimney to represent smoke.

14 Position the beanstalk root on background fabric. Pin in place.

15 Baste and stitch around each appliqué piece, close to the edge, using matching sewing thread. Using close zig-zag stitch, work around each appliqué piece again, over the previous stitching, again using matching thread.

16 Cut out 25 green leaves, varying the shapes by turning the patterns both ways and using different-textured fabrics.
17 On four leaves, finish the top edge, since these leaves will each form a pocket when stitched down. Work close zig-zag stitch along the edge for about 2in (5cm) between marks.

18 Pin, baste and stitch the leaves in place on the background, in the same way as the other appliqué pieces, leaving the top edges open so that the leaves form pockets. Stitch the pocket leaves at intervals up the stalk.

Terry Evans

19 Decorate the cottage. Cut trimming to represent flowers; pin, baste and sew in place along the base of the cottage. Pin, baste and sew trimming around the door and up the side wall of the cottage. Sew a bead to cottage door for doorknob.

20 Cut trimming into blossoms. Pin, baste and stitch blooms to bush.
21 Press on the wrong side.
22 For the border, cut out two strips, each $67 \times 7\frac{1}{2}$in (170×19cm), and two strips, each $44 \times 7\frac{1}{2}$in (112×19cm), from red poplin.

23 Pin, baste and stitch long border strips to each side of picture, matching long edges. Press strips away from picture.
24 Pin, baste and stitch short strips to top and base of picture in the same way.

25 Lay the picture/border right side up. Turn in and miter each corner. Pin, baste and stitch down each mitered corner. Trim away surplus fabric.
26 For backing, cut out one piece 66×44in (169×111cm) from light blue poplin. Position backing on picture/border, right sides together, matching all edges. Pin, baste and stitch all around, leaving a 10in (25cm) opening in the base edge. Trim corners and seams and turn quilt right side out.
27 Cut out two pieces of batting, each 65×43in (165×107cm). Place batting pieces together, matching all edges. Secure together with large basting stitches. Insert batting into quilt. Turn in edges and slip stitch them together.

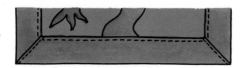

28 Lay the quilt flat. Pin, baste and stitch around inner edge of border, through all thicknesses, securing the batting in place.

Jack

Finished size
6in (15cm) tall.

Materials
   Three pipe cleaners
   Scraps of flesh-colored felt
   Embroidery floss for features
   Scrap of doll's hair or fine yarn
   5in (12cm) square of cotton fabric for shirt
   Scraps of blue and orange felt for clothes
   One small feather; fabric glue
   Small amount of stuffing
   Matching sewing thread

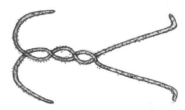

1 Twist two pipe cleaners together, 3in (7.5cm) from one end. Open out the remainder and bend out for shoulders and arms. Turn up $\frac{5}{8}$in (1.5cm) at opposite ends for feet.

2 Using the other pipe cleaner, twist the center into a circle for the head, twisting the remaining ends around the top of the arms.

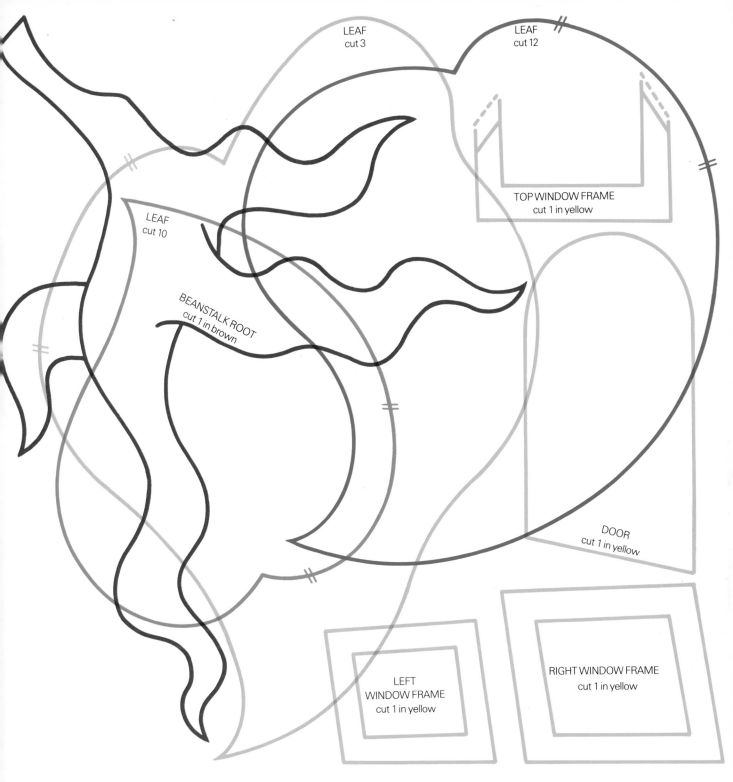

LEAF
cut 3

LEAF
cut 12

LEAF
cut 10

TOP WINDOW FRAME
cut 1 in yellow

BEANSTALK ROOT
cut 1 in brown

DOOR
cut 1 in yellow

LEFT
WINDOW FRAME
cut 1 in yellow

RIGHT WINDOW FRAME
cut 1 in yellow

3 Cut out two circles of flesh-colored felt for the head, slightly bigger than the pipe cleaner head. Place one circle on each side of pipe cleaner head and overcast together, stuffing as you work.
4 Embroider the features on one side of the head. Glue the hair in place.
5 Cut narrow strips of flesh-colored felt to cover arms and legs. Fold each strip in half over the pipe cleaner limbs and sew in place, taking a tiny seam allowance.
6 Pad out the body with stuffing and secure it in place by winding thread around the body.

7 For shirt, fold the fabric square in half. Place Jack on fabric with fold at top. Cut out a "T" shape, curving the underarm seams. Pin, baste and stitch the underarm seam, taking a tiny seam allowance. Slit down the center back of the shirt. Place the shirt over Jack. Run rows of gathering around the wrists and secure. Lap over the back opening and sew in place.
8 Cut out two 1¼in (3.5cm) squares of blue felt for trousers. Fold each square in half for trouser legs. Sew up long edges for ⅝in (1.5cm), taking a tiny seam allowance. Slip each leg over Jack, and overcast together at back and front.

9 For vest cut out a rectangle of orange felt 2¾ × 1¾in (7 × 4.5cm). Cut out two armholes ⅝in (1.5cm) in from long edges. Stitch shoulder seams. Curve lower front edges. Sew vest to Jack.
10 For hat cut out a 2¼in (6cm)-diameter circle for brim. Cut out the center of the circle to fit Jack's head. Cut out another circle ¾in (2cm) in diameter for hat crown. Cut a piece of felt ⅝in (1.5cm)-wide and overcast between brim and crown, trimming off excess felt to fit. Add a thin strip of orange felt and the feather to decorate the hat. Glue hat to Jack's head.

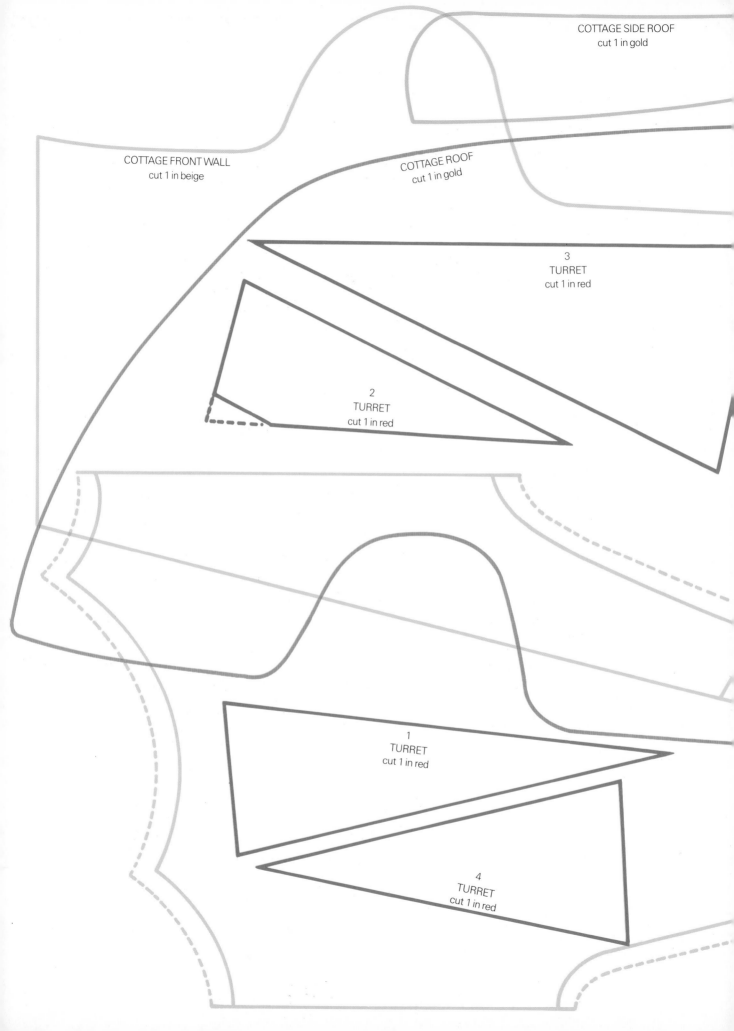

COTTAGE SIDE ROOF
cut 1 in gold

COTTAGE FRONT WALL
cut 1 in beige

COTTAGE ROOF
cut 1 in gold

3
TURRET
cut 1 in red

2
TURRET
cut 1 in red

1
TURRET
cut 1 in red

4
TURRET
cut 1 in red

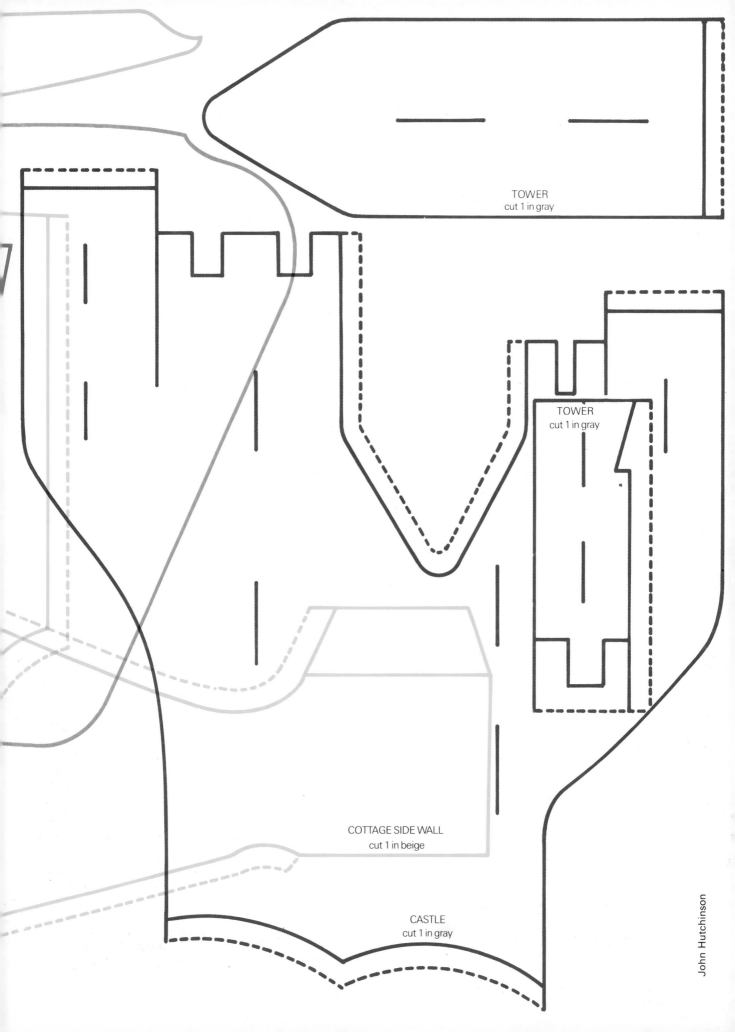

TOWER
cut 1 in gray

TOWER
cut 1 in gray

COTTAGE SIDE WALL
cut 1 in beige

CASTLE
cut 1 in gray

John Hutchinson

Finished size
60in (152cm) square.

Materials

Linen to make a piece 60in (152cm)
square
Five skeins of stranded embroidery
floss in pale green
Four skeins of stranded embroidery
floss in pale yellow
Small pearl-colored washable luster
beads
Matching sewing thread
8in (20cm)-diameter embroidery hoop
Tracing paper
Dressmaker's carbon paper

1 Seam and trim fabric to the correct size.

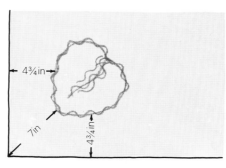

2 Trace the motif from the trace pattern shown below. Using dressmaker's carbon paper, mark the motif on the right side of the fabric. Place a motif in each corner of fabric, 7in (18cm) from the corner point and 4¾in (12cm) in from side edges.

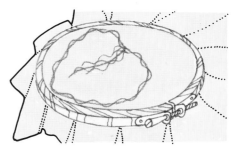

3 Place the motif area of fabric to be embroidered within the embroidery hoop and pull the fabric quite taut. Use three strands of embroidery floss throughout: green for leaves and stems and for sewing on beads, and yellow for flowers.

Brian Mayor

127

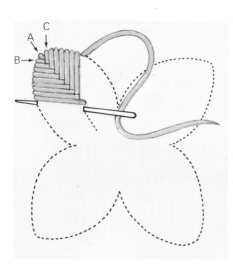

4 Work the flowers in fishbone stitch, completing one petal at a time. Bring the thread through the fabric at A and make a small straight stitch along the center line of the petal. Bring the thread through again at B and make a sloping stitch across the center line at the base of the first stitch. Bring the thread through at C and make a similar sloping stitch to overlap the previous stitch. Continue, working each side alternately, until the petal is filled.

5 Sew three beads in the center of each flower.

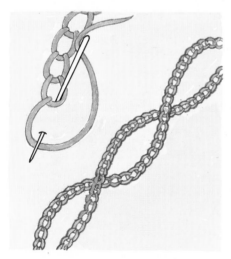

6 Work the stems in chain stitch, intertwining the lines of stitching. Bring the thread out at top of line and hold it

down with your left thumb. Insert the needle into the fabric where it last emerged and bring the needle point out a short distance away along the line of the design. Pull the thread through, keeping the working thread looped under the needle point.

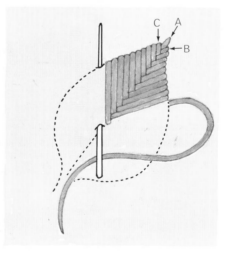

7 Work the leaves in fishbone stitch in the same way as the flower petals, but make the shape of each leaf more pointed by slanting the stitches at a sharper angle. Work each leaf so that the base is attached to the stem.

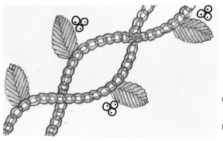

Terry Evans

8 Sew three beads in neat clusters around the motif as shown.
9 Work each motif in the same way in each of the four corners of the tablecloth.
10 Work single flowers at intervals between each corner motif along the sides of the tablecloth, $4\frac{3}{4}$in (12cm) from the edge. Work them in the same way as in the large flower motif, adding beads in the center.
11 To finish the edges of the tablecloth, work a scalloped edge on the sewing machine, using zig-zag stitch and pale green sewing thread. Trim away excess fabric to finish. Or finish by turning a double narrow hem all around the cloth, mitering the corners. Pin, baste and topstitch in place, using matching thread.
12 To remove all creases and enhance the embroidery, press the tablecloth on the wrong side with a steam iron, first placing it on folded bath towel.